C000181670

THE TRAFALGAR CAPTAINS

THEIR LIVES AND MEMORIALS

Colin White
and
The 1805 Club

CHATHAM PUBLISHING

LONDON

Dedicated
to the memory of
DEREK ALLEN
1946–2004

Note on transcriptions: Epitaphs have been transcribed
as closely as possible to the originals.
However, in some cases the constraints of the printed page
and the great length of the original lines
have made this impractical.

First published in Great Britain in 2005 by Chatham Publishing,
Lionel Leventhal Ltd, Park House, 1 Russell Gardens,
London NW11 9NN

British Library Cataloguing in Publication Data
White, Colin, 1951-
The Trafalgar captains : their lives and memorials
1.Nelson, Horatio Nelson, Viscount, 1758-1805 – Friends and associates
2. Great Britain. Royal Navy – Officers – Biography
3. Great Britain. Royal Navy – Officers – Monuments
4. Trafalgar, Battle of, 1805
I. Title II 1805 Club
2.359' .0092241
ISBN 1 86176 247 X

Typeset and designed by Sally Geeve
Printed and bound in China

CONTENTS

CONTRIBUTORS

Leslie Bennett (LB) is a member of The 1805 Club, The Nelson Society, the Society for Nautical Research and the Navy Records Society. He has a biography of Vice-Admiral Sir Henry Blackwood in final stages of publication, with the title *Nelson's Eyes*.

Sim C Comfort (SCC) runs the short-run publishing house, Sim Comfort Associates, which has reprinted *Naval Architecture* and *Rigging & Seamanship* by David Steel, and James Jenkins' *Naval Achievements*. His first book, *Forget Me Not*, deals with sailor-made engraved coins.

Anthony Cross (AJC) runs the Warwick Leadlay Gallery, Greenwich. He has published catalogues on a Nelsonian theme, and acted as picture editor and author to the *Nelson Almanac*. He has broadcast on BBC Radio 4's 'Making History' as well as contributing to several documentaries about Nelson.

John Curtis (JC) was the Librarian of Lloyd's of London and in 1987 was entrusted with the curatorship of the Lloyd's Nelson Collection. Closely involved in the Trafalgar Captains Memorial Project, he has been responsible for much research, and the recording of the graves and monuments.

Charles Alan Fremantle (CAF) is a direct descendant of Admiral Thomas Francis Fremantle, and himself a former naval officer. His remarkable unbroken family tradition of naval service finally ended in 1988, after 211 years, when his daughter Naomi left the WRNR.

John Goddard (JG) has carried out research for Captain K J Douglas-Morris's leading work *Naval Medals 1793-1856* and he has since contributed articles to the Journal of the Orders and Medals Research Society, the monthly magazine *Medal News* and The 1805 Club's *Trafalgar Chronicle*.

John Gwyther (JRG) was drawn to Nelson from a long association with Sardinia. He is an honorary member of the historical society of the island of La Maddalena, and was closely linked to the restoration of the silver crucifix and candlesticks donated by Nelson to the island's parish church.

Stephen Howarth (SWRH) has published fourteen major works on such diverse topics as the Koh-i-Noor diamond, the Knights Templar, and the international oil industry; but naval history remains his first love. With his late father David Howarth he co-wrote *Nelson: The Immortal Memory*.

Nick Slope (NS) is an archaeologist and naval historian and has written and broadcast widely on aspects of Nelson's Navy. He has recently been responsible for the rescue excavation of British service personnel buried on Nelson's Island, Aboukir, Egypt. He is Chairman of the Nelson Society.

Peter Warwick (PW) has had a lifelong interest in Nelson and is a committee member of The Society for Nautical Research. He is also Chairman of The 1805 Club and Vice-Chairman of the Official Nelson Commemorations Committee, co-ordinating The Trafalgar Festival.

Colin White (CSW) is a leading Nelson scholar with three books on Nelson to his credit and two more – *Nelson: The New Letters* and *Nelson the Admiral* – published in 2005. He is currently working at the National Maritime Museum as curator for their 2005 exhibition *Nelson and Napoleon*.

Gerald William White (GWW) developed a special interest in the history of the RN while at Dartmouth. He is chairing the New Trafalgar Dispatch, an event that will recreate the delivery by Lieutenant Lapenotiere of Admiral Collingwood's Trafalgar Dispatch to the Admiralty in London in 1805.

Anthony Wozencroft (AW) was a former Project Officer and Council member of The 1805 Club and has been closely associated with the conservation of graves and the placing of commemorative plaques at a number of important sites. He is Yeoman Guide at The Old Royal Naval College Greenwich.

RECORDERS & RESEARCHERS

Grateful thanks are due to the following people who very kindly gave their time to research and provide information on the graves and monuments that are opposite their names.

Baker, Elizabeth	Cooke (Donhead St Andrew)
	Digby
Birkbeck, Sally	Codrington (Brookwood)
	Laforey
Bland, Frank	Dundas
Brockman, Stephen	Moorsom
Curtis, John	Codrington (Pylos)
	King
Draisey, John	Stockham
	Young
Fraser, Barry	Mansfield
	Rutherfurd
	Codrington (Eaton Square)
Fremantle, Charles	Fremantle (Malta)
Grigg, Franklin	Hennah
Henderson, Alison	Bullen
Hilton, J David	Harvey
	Rotheram
Howarth, Stephen	Prowse
Hughes, Terry	Bayntun
	Berry
	Hargood
	Tyler
Le Quesne, Leslie	Blackwood (Westminster Abbey)
	Hope (Westminster Abbey)
McCann, Brian	Collingwood (Newcastle and Tynemouth)
	Cumby (Heighington)
Milton–Thompson, Godfrey	Lapenotiere
McKay, Jean	Durham
Mogey, Sammy	Blackwood (Killyleagh)
Phillips, Lawrence	Cumby (Pembroke)
Richards, Basil	Moorsom
Scragg, Doreen	Fremantle (Malta)
Sharp, Richard	Grindall
Smart, Christopher	Codrington (Dodington)
Wadsworth, Revd Peter	Redmill
Warwick, Peter	Morris
	Codrington (Brookwood)
White, Bill	Capel
White, Colin	Codrington (St Paul's Cathedral)
	Collingwood (St Paul's Cathedral)
	Cooke (St Paul's Cathedral)
	Duff (St Paul's Cathedral)
	Nelson (St Paul's Cathedral)
	Northesk (St Paul's Cathedral)
Wozencroft, Anthony	Hardy
	King

EDITOR'S FOREWORD

Nelson's immortal fame tends to overshadow the memory of those who served with him and this is particularly true of the men who commanded the ships that fought at Trafalgar. Collingwood and Hardy apart, most of the other British senior officers at the battle are now completely unknown.

In early 2003, the council of The 1805 Club began considering ways of marking the bicentenary of Trafalgar. The club has two main aims: to encourage research into the Georgian Royal Navy and to restore the graves and monuments of people associated with the Navy of that time. Recognising the need to rescue the Trafalgar Captains from obscurity, and to celebrate their achievements, the council decided to launch the Trafalgar Captains Memorial Project as its principal initiative for 2005. The aim of the project was to locate, record and, where necessary, restore the graves and monuments of all those who commanded ships, or flew their flags, at Trafalgar.

The wording of that aim was carefully chosen. Early on, it was agreed that the project should include not only those who held the rank of admiral or captain but also the lieutenants who commanded ships – including the two who took over command during the battle, when their captains were killed. As a result, the project has encompassed thirty-eight men – three admirals, twenty-nine captains and six lieutenants.

Two years later, the first two stages of the project are complete. Thanks to the efforts of a large team of researchers and recorders – most of them members of the club – we have located the site of the grave and/or monument of every Trafalgar senior officer. The recording process also is complete: each grave and monument that has survived has been visited and meticulously described by members of our team. Additionally, the club has commissioned professional photographer Matt Prince to produce a unique visual record of all the surviving graves and monuments and a stunning collection of over three hundred images has resulted. The restoration stage of the project, involving work on seven graves and monuments, is dependent on sufficient funds being raised to finance the necessary works. The Club is actively seeking sponsorship for this stage and would be glad to hear from any person, or organisation, willing to assist.

It was always the club's intention to make the results of the project as widely available as possible and this book is a key part of that process. The voluminous records of the graves and monuments gathered by our team have been expertly collated by the club secretary, John Curtis, to create a comprehensive list, and this has been supplemented by a small selection of Matt Prince's superb photographs. Because this book is intended to honour the admirals and captains who fought with Nelson, rather than the great man himself, we have decided not to unbalance it by including all the many Nelson monuments. He is represented here simply by his tomb in St Paul's Cathedral and by the national monument to him, also in St Paul's. A complete list, with illustrations, of all the other Nelson monuments, in Britain and overseas, may be found in the comprehensive review by Flora Fraser in *The Nelson Companion*, full details of which appear in the bibliography.

Additionally, short biographies of each officer – again, with the exception of Nelson, who is being more than sufficiently 'biographied' just at present – have been researched and written by members of The 1805 Club. These are based mainly on printed material, notably the *Dictionary of National Biography*, *The Trafalgar Roll* and Marshall's *Naval Biography*. However, twelve of the men featured in this book do not appear at all in the new DNB, while others have only very short entries; *The Trafalgar Roll* offers only outline career summaries in many cases and Marshall deals only with those who were still alive in the 1830s. Moreover, original research by some of the participating authors has enabled them to fill a number of gaps in the existing material and also to offer some answers to hitherto unsolved questions. As a result, this is the most complete record available of the service of the men who commanded at Trafalgar.

It must be emphasised, however, that this is not another book about the Battle of Trafalgar. Like Nelson, the battle is currently being much studied and written about, in books and conference papers, and many new ideas and theories are emerging. For those who wish to explore the actual fighting in more detail, a list of our main sources has been provided in the appendices.

Nor is this a book about all those who fought at Trafalgar. Again, much new research is currently under way thanks to the work of Pam and Derek Ayshford who have assembled the personal details of every man who fought on the British side and whose remarkable 'Trafalgar Roll' can now be obtained in CD-ROM form.

Instead, this book deliberately concentrates on a particular group of officers, celebrates their achievements, and pinpoints the places where they are memorialised. The hope of all of us who have been involved in the Trafalgar Captains Memorial Project is that, as a result of our work, these gallant men will never be allowed to fall into obscurity again. We hope that, instead, the communities among whom they now rest will claim them, and honour them – and not just in 2005, but for many years to come.

Colin White
Portsmouth, 1 January 2005

ACKNOWLEDGEMENTS

The council of The 1805 Club would like to express warm thanks and appreciation to all those who have been involved in the production of this book.

First: the team of researchers and recorders who collected the information about the graves and monuments that form the basis of the second section. Their names appear in the list on page 4 but we would like to thank especially John Draisey of the Devon Records Office who has been so tirelessly helpful in locating the whereabouts of the now vanished graves of Stockham and Young. Additionally, we would like to express special thanks to Matt Prince whose superb photographic record has so brilliantly complemented and enhanced the written records.

Second: all those involved in the running of the various churches that Matt Prince and our recorders have visited – clergy, churchwardens and laity. Everywhere we have met with a level of kindness and practical help that has been truly heart-warming. A particular thank you is due to Duncan Smith and the electricians at St Paul's Cathedral who gave their time without limit on the day before the big press launch of the newly-restored west front. We are also most grateful to the Dean and Chapter of Westminster Abbey for allowing us to reproduce their own photographs of the memorials in their care.

Third: sincere thanks are due to the various authors of the biographical essays, all of them members of The 1805 Club and all of whom have given their services free. Their details appear on page 4 and they are identified by their initials at the end of the essays they have contributed. Special thanks are due to Sim Comfort who has also written about the Trafalgar Awards on pages 123–5 and who has supplied a number of the illustrations from his superb private collection. Other illustrations have been supplied by Anthony Cross and the Warwick Leadlay Gallery in Greenwich, that essential emporium for all lovers of Nelson and his Navy. We are also grateful to David Taylor of the National Maritime Museum and Stephen Courtney of the Royal Naval Museum for assistance in locating the remaining illustrations.

Finally, the editor would like to thank his fellow members of the Trafalgar Captains Memorial Project Committee, whose names and responsibilities are listed on page 128. And he knows the other members of the committee will agree with him when he singles out for special recognition Club Secretary John Curtis. He has acted as the archivist for the project since its inception and kept in touch with all the recorders and researchers as their work proceeded. His meticulously-kept records have formed the bedrock of both sections of this book and he has been solely responsible for compiling the entries on the graves and monuments.

Location of Graves &

ENGLAND

BATH
Bayntun
Berry
Hargood

BILDESTON (Suffolk)
Rotheram

BRIGHTON
Laforey

COSGROVE (Northants)
Moorsom

DODINGTON (Glos)
Codrington

DONHEAD ST ANDREW (Wilts)
Cooke

EASTCHURCH (Kent)
King

EXETER
Stockham
Young

HEIGHINGTON (Co Durham)
Cumby

HEMPSTEAD (Essex)
Harvey

HURST (Berks)
Dundas

LONDON
  Eaton Sq
  Codrington
  Greenwich
  Hardy
  Kensal Green
  Capel
  St Pancras
  Prowse

St Paul's Cathedral
Nelson (tomb & statue)
Collingwood (tomb & statue)
Northesk
Codrington
Cooke
Duff
Westminster Abbey
Blackwood
Hope
Westminster (St Margaret's)
Rutherfurd

MARLOW (Bucks)
Morris

MENHENIOT (Cornwall)
Lapenotiere

MINTERNE MAGNA (Dorset)
Digby

MORPETH (Northumberland)
Collingwood

NEWCASTLE-UPON-TYNE
Collingwood

PLYMOUTH
Pellew
Pilfold

ROCHESTER (Kent)
Mansfield

SOUTHAMPTON (2 locations)
Bullen

STEVENAGE (Herts)
Redmill

TREGONY (Cornwall)
Hennah

TYNEMOUTH (N Tyneside)
Collingwood

WICKHAM (Hants)
Grindall

N IRELAND

Killyleagh (Co Down)
Blackwood

SCOTLAND

UPPER LARGO (Fife)
Durham

WALES

PEMBROKE DOCK
Cumby

St Nicholas (Glamorg
Tyler

OVERSEAS

GREECE
Pylos
Codrington

ITALY
Naples
Fremantle

MALTA
Valetta
Fremantle

BURIED AT SEA

Off Cape Trafalgar
Cooke
Duff

Off Bermuda
Conn

Memorials

Upper Largo ✝

Morpeth ✝✝ Tynemouth
Newcastle-upon-Tyne

Killyleagh ✝

Heighington ✝

✝ Cosgrove

Bildeston
✝ ✝

Dodington   Hempstead ✝
Pembroke Dock   ✝   ✝ Stevenage ✝
            St Nicholas ✝   Marlow ✝
                Bath ✝   Hurst ✝   ✝
                        ✝ ✝ Eastchurch
            Donhead St Andrew   LONDON ✝✝
                        Rochester
    Exeter ✝   ✝ Southampton   Brighton
Menheniot ✝ ✝ Minterne Magna   ✝ ✝
Tregony ✝ ✝ Plymouth   Wickham ✝

9

INTRODUCTION
by COLIN WHITE

The British fleet at Trafalgar was hurriedly created, almost from scratch. Ships were drawn from various sources to meet the emergency: some were summoned from the Mediterranean, others detached from the Channel fleet; yet others were rushed out from the English dockyards. Even when the fleet began to assemble off Cadiz, in September 1805, its composition was never static. Ships were constantly arriving, while others were being sent off on special missions or to replenish their stores.

If the selection of the ships that made up the fleet that actually fought the French and Spanish on 21 October owed more to chance than to planning, then the choice of the captains who commanded at the battle was also to a considerable degree arbitrary. As a result, they can fairly be regarded as a representative cross-section of the Royal Navy in 1805 and when we examine them, and their careers, some interesting patterns emerge.

Excluding the three admirals, and the two lieutenants who took command during the battle when their captains were killed, the average age was 41. Three were over 50: Richard Grindall (55), Edward Rotheram (53) and William Prowse (52). The youngest in the fleet was Bladen Capel of the *Phoebe* at 29 but that was not unusually young for a frigate captain, especially one with as much family influence as Capel. The surprising youngster, at 31, was Richard King of the battleship *Achilles* – surprising, that is, until it is remembered that he was the son of an admiral and married to the daughter of another!

They came from all over Great Britain. Devon and Cornwall were the best represented, with seven of those whose birthplaces are known, hailing from the two western counties, including Israel Pellew and William Hennah. There were also three from Northumbria – Cuthbert Collingwood, his flag captain Edward Rotheram, and Charles Bullen of the *Britannia* – and three Scots – Lord Northesk, George Duff and Thomas Dundas. Ireland was represented by Henry Blackwood, the Isle of Man by Robert Young and Yorkshire by Robert Moorsom. There were even two Americans, both of whom had been born when their states were still British colonies. Francis Laforey hailed from Virginia and William Rutherfurd from Wilmington, North Carolina – his mother was the widow of one of the colony's former governors, Gabriel Johnson.

Their social background was equally diverse. At the upper end of the scale six – that is, rather less than 20% – were from the aristocracy. Only Northesk was a peer in his own right: he was the seventh Earl. The others were mostly younger sons of peers and baronets. Bladen Capel was the youngest son of the Earl of Essex; George Hope the grandson of the Earl of Hopetoun; Henry Blackwood, the seventh son of a baronet. Henry Digby was the eldest son of the Honourable and Very Reverend William Digby, Dean of Durham and Chaplain

Ordinary to King George III.

All the rest were from various branches of the middle class. Thomas Fremantle's father was a landowner, as was Philip Durham's. Henry Bayntun's father had been a diplomat; Edward Berry and Cuthbert Collingwood were the sons of merchants; William Hennah, like Nelson, the son of a parson; George Duff the son of a solicitor and Edward Rotheram the son of a doctor. Finally, and, unsurprisingly, about a third of them came from service families. Richard King and Francis Laforey were the sons of admirals; Israel Pellew, William Cumby and James Morris of captains. William Hargood's father had been a purser and John Cooke's a cashier at the Admiralty. Charles Tyler was the son of an Army captain.

Their previous experience of active service varied considerably. A clear majority – twenty-one in all – had taken part in a fleet action before. Some had served at Rodney's great victory over the French at the Battle of the Saintes in April 1783; others at Howe's victory at the Glorious First of June 1794 – Edward Codrington, for example, was Howe's signal lieutenant. He was sent home with the admiral's duplicate dispatches, thus earning his promotion to commander. William Prowse fared less well: the sixth lieutenant in HMS *Barfleur*, commanded by Cuthbert Collingwood, he had been so badly wounded in the leg that it had to be amputated. Edward Rotheram had been first lieutenant of the *Culloden*, thus winning his promotion to commander. Charles Bullen had won his promotion to the same rank, when he served as first lieutenant of HMS *Monmouth* at the ferocious battle of Camperdown fought against the Dutch on 11 October 1797

On the other hand, of the battleship captains only six – Edward Berry, Philip Durham, Thomas Fremantle, Robert Redmill, Charles Tyler and Richard Grindall – had commanded battleships in a fleet action before. Additionally, Thomas Hardy John Conn and John Cooke had commanded small ships at a major action. Hardy had commanded the brig *Mutine* at the Nile in August 1798 and had been present as a volunteer in Nelson's flagship HMS *Elephant* at Copenhagen in April 1801. Conn had commanded a bomb vessel at the Copenhagen and Cooke had been in command of a fireship at the Glorious First of June in 1794.

In all, ten of the battleship captains – and twelve out of the whole Trafalgar fleet – had previously served with Nelson. Of these, five ships and captains had been with him at various stages during the long campaign of 1803/5 and the great chase to the West Indies. These were: Thomas Hardy of the *Victory*, whose close association with Nelson in fact went back over ten years, Henry Bayntun of the *Leviathan*, John Conn of the *Dreadnought* (although he had commanded the *Canopus* in the Mediterranean), William Hargood of the *Belleisle* and Israel Pellew of the *Conqueror*. Additionally, Francis Laforey in the *Spartiate* had joined Nelson in the West Indies in June 1805 and had taken part in the return voyage in pursuit of the Combined Fleet. Of the frigate captains, Thomas

Bladen Capel of the *Phoebe* was one of Nelson's particular young protégés having served as lieutenant in the *Vanguard* at the Battle of the Nile and had taken home the admiral's duplicate dispatches. He later joined Nelson in the Mediterranean, in 1803, in command of the frigate *Phoebe* and so distinguished himself that, when Nelson left the Mediterranean in chase of the Combined Fleet in May 1805, he put Capel in command of a small squadron of frigates left behind to protect British trade.

Two other captains had served with Nelson in the earlier campaign in the Mediterranean of 1798–1800. George Hope, now commanding the battleship HMS *Defence* had then been a frigate captain. Henry Blackwood of the *Euryalus* was a particular favourite. He had first caught Nelson's eye in 1800 when he contributed, in his frigate HMS *Penelope,* to the capture of the French battleship *Guillaume Tell.* Additionally, Charles Tyler had been a fellow-captain with Nelson in the Mediterranean at the outset of the war with France and had commanded HMS *Warrior* during the Baltic campaign of 1801.

The remaining two were, like Hardy, old and trusted friends and colleagues, members of the original 'Band of Brothers'. Edward Berry had served with Nelson in the Mediterranean in the mid-1790s, first as his first lieutenant in HMS *Captain* and then as his flag captain in the *Vanguard.* Thomas Fremantle had been at his side when Nelson took part in hand-to-hand fighting against a Spanish gunboat at Cadiz in June 1797 and again at Santa Cruz de Tenerife the following month where both men had been severely wounded in the right arm. At Copenhagen, he had commanded the battleship *Ganges* just ahead of Nelson's flagship HMS *Elephant* in the British line.

Everyone expected the Combined Fleet to come out soon and so when Nelson took command, he was aware that he might not have long to mould this

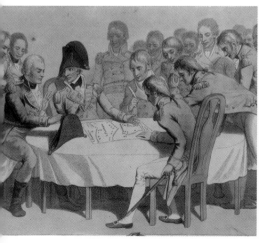

The Trafalgar Briefing, Nelson's cabin in HMS Victory *29 September 1805.*

disparate group of men, with their widely differing backgrounds and professional experience, into a unified fighting team. Characteristically, he set about doing it with a combination of hospitality, inspiration and a display of energy. Arriving on 28 September, he immediately held two dinner parties – one on the 29th, his forty-seventh birthday; the other the following day. As is well-known, he took the opportunity to brief all his new subordinates verbally about his battle plan, reducing some of them to tears of excitement.

Soon, a stream of orders was issuing from the *Victory*'s great cabin covering all aspects of the running of the fleet. Nelson's old friend and colleague Thomas Fremantle approved of the new edge that Nelson had given to the fleet's activities, remarking to his wife, 'the energy and activity on board the *Victory* will make those who are slack keep a much better lookout and preserve better discipline.' Nor was it only Nelson's old comrades who approved. Edward Codrington told his wife, 'Lord Nelson is arrived. A sort of general joy has been the consequence.' And George Duff wrote home, 'he is certainly the pleasantest admiral I ever served with.' Both men had, quite independently, given orders for their ships to be repainted in the same 'chequer-board' livery as Nelson's Mediterranean ships

Most of the captains, and especially those who had served with Nelson before, performed very well in the ensuing battle and showed by their actions that they had understood the spirit as well as the letter of Nelson's plan – and moreover that they were consciously copying his style of leadership. This was seen even before the action began, when some of them sought ways to pass on to their subordinates the inspiration they had received from the admiral. According to James Martin, one of his sailors, Thomas Fremantle went round the ship during the long approach to battle, visiting his men at their action stations and told them, 'our Native Land and all that was Dear to us Hung upon a balance….happy the Man who Boldly Ventured his Life in such a cause.' Charles Mansfield called all hands onto the quarterdeck and said,

I trust that This day or to Morrow will prove the most glorious our country ever saw…for my own part I pledge myself to the officers & ships company never to quit the ship I may get alongside of till either she strikes or sinks.

He was echoing – perhaps consciously – Nelson's famous injunction in the memorandum he had circulated to all his captains a fortnight before,

'*No captain can do very wrong if he places his ship alongside that of an enemy.*'

Once the fighting began, some captains – especially Edward Codrington, Israel Pellew, Henry Bayntun and Charles Tyler – were highly effective and mobile. They ranged among the French and Spanish ships, assisting comrades who were in difficulty and, as Nelson had intended, combining with other British ships to bring overwhelming force to bear on isolated enemy ships. So, for example, Pellew first forced the *Bucentaure* to surrender, then assisted in the capture of the *Santissima Trinidad* and finally helped to reduce *L'Intrepide* to a wreck. Others, like William Hargood of the *Belleisle*, John Cooke of the *Bellerophon* and George Duff in the *Mars*, found themselves fighting lone battles against superior odds – gallantry for which Cooke and Duff both paid with their lives.

There were, however, a few captains who did not appear to understand Nelson's intentions, or who did not feel inclined to follow them. Neither Robert Redmill in the *Polyphemus* nor Richard Grindall in the *Prince* appear to have made very strenuous efforts to get their ships into action and Collingwood's flag captain, Edward Rotheram, later said of Grindall that he 'behaved notoriously ill at the Trafalgar action.' Robert Moorsom later went so far as to remark 'I am not certain that our mode of attack was the best,' but he at least had some excuse for his scepticism. Having arrived early in the midst of the fighting, not far astern of Collingwood, he found himself surrounded by three enemy ships, with which he fought a gallant but very bloody duel for over half an hour, suffering almost 80 casualties before Philip Durham was able to come to his rescue in HMS *Defiance*.

Moorsom was wounded in the face during the action, one of ten casualties among the senior British officers. Of the admirals, only Northesk escaped unscathed: Nelson was killed and Collingwood was badly bruised in the thigh by a splinter and injured in his back by the wind of a passing shot. Captains Cooke and Duff were killed and Hargood, Tyler, Morris, Durham, Pellew and Moorsom wounded. Cooke's death was a remarkable mirror-image of Nelson's – he was struck in the chest by a sniper's bullet during a close-quarter's duel with *L'Aigle*, which had on board a large contingent of soldiers. There was another, even closer, reflection of the scene in the *Victory*: only shortly before Cooke's death, the First Lieutenant, William Cumby had pointed out to his captain that his epaulettes made him an obvious target. Like Nelson, Cooke had refused to make any change to his habitual dress.

Musket balls also accounted for the injuries suffered by Charles Tyler and James Morris, both of whom were hit in the leg. Tyler's wound was so serious that at one point he thought it might be mortal: his epitaph records that 'it was nearly his fate to participate' in Nelson's 'glorious end'. Morris applied a crude tourniquet and went on commanding his ship; but he lost so much blood that he almost fainted at the end of the day. The captains therefore suffered a 30% casualty rate – much higher than the lieutenants, who suffered losses of only 19%, and only marginally lower than the boatswains, who lost 33% of their number. These rates reflect the relative exposure of the positions in which the men in these different ranks were stationed. The boatswains were usually on the completely open fo'c'sles; admirals and captains by contrast were rather better protected on the quarterdeck, having the poop behind them and hammock nettings all around, although they were still quite exposed, especially to small arms fire from the rigging of an opponent. By contrast, lieutenants were dispersed all round the ship and some of them served on the much safer gun decks.

Following the battle, friend and foe alike faced the challenge of the great storm that burst over them and here all the captains seem to have performed with comparable skill and courage. William Rutherford and his men in HMS *Swiftsure* had reached the battle only during its closing stages: in time to come to the aid of the dismasted *Belleisle* and then to assist in rescuing the crew of the blazing French battleship *Achille*. During the storm they performed heroic feats of seamanship and lifesaving: attempting first to save the wallowing wreck of the *Redoutable*, formerly the *Victory's* opponent and then, when this was no longer possible, rescuing many of her crew in heaving seas and high winds at great risk to their own lives. The storm was also an opportunity for the frigates, by tradition only spectators in a fleet action, to play an active role. Thomas Dundas's *Naiad* managed to save the badly-damaged *Belleisle* and tow her into Gibraltar. Capel, in the *Phoebe* performed the same service for the captured French *Swiftsure* until, on 24 October, Collingwood ordered the prizes to be to scuttled.

George Duff and John Cooke were buried at sea but Nelson's body, preserved in a barrel of brandy, was carried home to Britain in HMS *Victory* and accorded a State Funeral with full heraldic pomp. Eight of the Trafalgar captains were present at the ceremonies and took part in the elaborate processions on the River Thames, through the streets of London and in St Paul's Cathedral. Eliab Harvey, by then promoted to rear admiral, was one of the pall bearers, while his former comrades carried various items of heraldic paraphernalia. Thomas Hardy and Henry Bayntun bore the allegorical Banner of Emblems, with its figure of Britannia mourning the dead hero; Robert Moorson carried the Great Banner; Francis Laforey the Standard; Philip Durham Nelson's personal banner as a Knight of the Bath and Edward Rotheram the 'Guidon' (a heraldic pennant usually carried by cavalry regiments). Henry Blackwood was trainbearer to the Chief Mourner, Admiral of the Fleet Sir Peter Parker, who had given the young Nelson his all-important promotion to post captain in 1779. The newly-promoted Captain William Cumby was also present at the service but did not have an official role.

Following Trafalgar, many of the captains did not see action again. Some, like Richard Grindall and Robert Redmill retired from active service at once: others went on serving but without hearing a gun fired in anger. Only Edward Codrington eventually commanded a fleet in action – and he had to wait until 1827 for his opportunity at the battle of Navarino, when he was in charge of a combined British, French and Russian fleet in a battle against the Turks. Twenty-two of the surviving captains went on to become admirals but, since promotion to flag rank was by seniority rather than merit, this was not a particularly noteworthy achievement. Twelve actually flew their flags afloat as Commanders-in-Chief – and here merit does seem to have played a part, for they were usually the ones who had performed best at the battle. So, for example, Charles Tyler became C-in-C, Cape of Good Hope in 1812; Philip Durham, C-in-C Leeward Isles in 1813 and Richard King, C-in-C West Indies in 1818. Thomas Fremantle and Edward Codrington followed their former leader in command of the Mediterranean in 1819 and 1827 respectively, although Fremantle managed to enjoy the position for only a year before dying in Naples. Thomas Hardy reached the highest office of all, becoming First Sea Lord in 1830. By then, ten of his former comrades had already joined Nelson,

Cooke and Duff and, by the time Hardy himself died, in 1839, another eleven had gone. The last to survive were Bladen Capel and Charles Bullen, who died within four months of each other in 1853, Bullen being the last to go in July.

Even in their memorials the captains remained strikingly disparate. Ten were given very simple epitaphs: often with just their name, rank and dates, such as Henry Baytun, Thomas Dundas or William Hennah. Others were much more elaborately memorialised: such as William Hargood with an intricate plaque in Bath Abbey, or Henry Blackwood with similarly elaborate plaques, both in his own church in Killyleagh, County Down, and in Westminster Abbey. In the case of twelve of the captains, no mention at all was made of Trafalgar on their memorials: in most of the others, it features prominently. For example, William Cumby's elaborate epitaph details all the ships to which the *Bellerophon* was opposed in the battle and then continues:

He nobly maintained the unequal contest, displaying in this critical position a skill and valour worthy of that eventful day and animating by his example the victorious efforts of his gallant crew.

The epitaphs of five captains make special mention of their closeness to Nelson: Thomas Hardy and Edward Berry as might be expected; but also Charles Tyler, Henry Digby and Eliab Harvey. Most poignant, perhaps, is the plaque erected in memory of her husband in St Andrew's Church Donhead, by Louisa Cooke:

Be merciful to her O God who bends
And mourns the best of Husbands, Fathers, Friends.

However the rest of the memorial lovingly demonstrates how proud she was of her husband's achievements; by contrast Margaretta Morris made no mention at all of her husband's naval service, preferring instead to highlight that 'He was a sincere Christian in his belief and practice.'

The day after the battle Vice Admiral Cuthbert Collingwood penned an eloquent General Order to his fleet expressing his thanks to his officers and men for their services:

but where can I find language to express my sentiments of the valour and skill displayed by the Officers, the Seamen and Marines in the Battle with the enemy where every individual appeared an Hero, on whom the glory of his Country depended.

'Every individual appeared an hero.' Collingwood was surely right, in the immediate aftermath of such a victory, to insist that all had performed equally well. But two hundred years later it is possible to acknowledge that the Trafalgar captains were not a faultless elite of equally talented men. Rather, they were a true cross-section of the Royal Navy in which they served, with fascinating contrasts in their backgrounds, abilities and levels of performance. As we approach the bicentenary of their great joint achievement it is a timely moment to allow them emerge as individuals and to celebrate their rich diversity.

'Hoisting 'England Expects'' by Thomas Davidson. Nelson stands with Hardy and Blackwood on the Victory's poop as the famous signal is hoisted. William Prowse is shown right background with the telescope, c.11.30 on 21 October 1805.

'The Battle of Trafalgar'. The two English lines are clearly depicted. By Thomas Luny.

The ships and their captains

			Killed	Wounded
WEATHER COLUMN				
Victory	100	Vice Admiral Lord Nelson Captain Thomas Hardy	57	102
Temeraire	98	Captain Eliab Harvey	47	76
Neptune	98	Captain Thomas Fremantle	10	34
Leviathan	74	Captain Henry Bayntun	4	22
Britannia	100	Rear Admiral Lord Northesk Captain Charles Bullen	10	42
Conqueror	74	Captain Israel Pellew	3	9
Africa	64	Captain Henry Digby	18	44
Agamemnon	64	Captain Sir Edward Berry	2	8
Ajax	74	Lieutenant John Pilfold	2	9
Orion	74	Captain Edward Codrington	1	23
Minotaur	74	Captain Charles Mansfield	3	22
Spartiate	74	Captain Sir Francis Laforey	3	20
LEE COLUMN				
Royal Sovereign	100	Vice Admiral Cuthbert Collingwood Captain Edward Rotheram	47	94
Belleisle	74	Captain William Hargood	33	93
Mars	74	Captain George Duff Lieutenant William Hennah	29	69
Tonnant	80	Captain Charles Tyler	26	50
Bellerophon	74	Captain John Cooke Lieutenant William Cumby	27	123
Colossus	74	Captain James Morris	40	160
Achilles	74	Captain Richard King	13	59
Dreadnought	98	Captain John Conn	7	26
Polyphemus	64	Captain Robert Redmill	2	4
Revenge	74	Captain Robert Moorsom	28	51
Swiftsure	74	Captain William Rutherfurd	9	8
Defiance	74	Captain Philip Durham	17	53
Thunderer	74	Lieutenant John Stockham	4	12
Defence	74	Captain George Hope	7	29
Prince	98	Captain Richard Grindall	0	0
FRIGATES AND OTHER VESSELS				
Euryalus	36	Captain the Hon Henry Blackwood		
Naiad	38	Captain Thomas Dundas		
Phoebe	36	Captain the Hon Thomas Bladen Capel		
Sirius	36	Captain William Prowse		
Pickle	10	Lieutenant John Lapenotiere		
Entreprenante	8	Lieutenant Robert Young		

N

WIND

Sirius
Naiad
Britar
(Nort
Pickle
Phoebe
Entreprenante
Agamemnon
Orion
Prince
Minotaur
Co
Spartiate
Achille
Thunderer
Dreadnought
Revenge
Defence
Defiance
Polyphemus
Swiftsure

THE BATTLE OF TRAFALGAR
21 October 1805

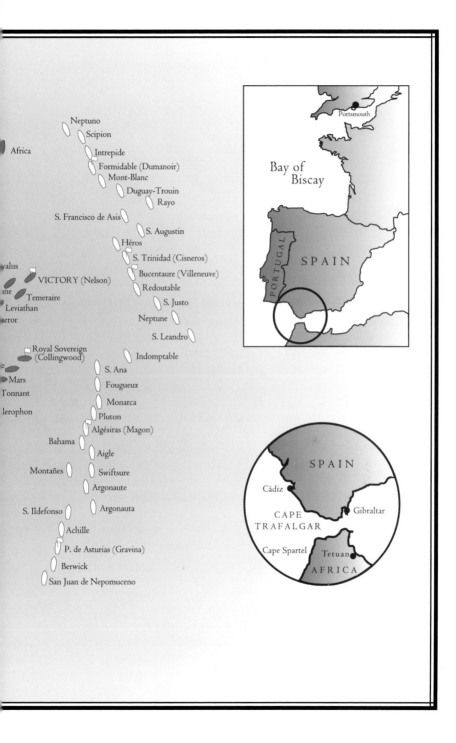

Neptuno
Scipion
Intrepide
Formidable (Dumanoir)
Mont-Blanc
Duguay-Trouin
Rayo
Africa
S. Francisco de Asis
S. Augustin
Héros
S. Trinidad (Cisneros)
Bucentaure (Villeneuve)
Redoutable
S. Justo
Neptune
S. Leandro
Royal Sovereign
(Collingwood)
Indomptable
VICTORY (Nelson)
Temeraire
Leviathan
eror
yalus
ine
Mars
S. Ana
Tonnant
Fougueux
lerophon
Monarca
Pluton
Algésiras (Magon)
Bahama
Aigle
Montañes
Swiftsure
Argonaute
S. Ildefonso
Argonauta
Achille
P. de Asturias (Gravina)
Berwick
San Juan de Nepomuceno

Portsmouth

Bay of
Biscay

SPAIN

PORTUGAL

SPAIN
Cádiz
CAPE
TRAFALGAR
Gibraltar
Cape Spartel
Tetuan
AFRICA

HENRY WILLIAM BAYNTUN
(1766–1840)
Captain HMS *Leviathan*

Although Henry Bayntun was one of Sir John Jervis's pupils, his professional relationship with Nelson did not begin until 1804 when Bayntun, in the *Leviathan*, joined the Mediterranean squadron off Toulon. The *Leviathan* was also under Nelson's orders for the chase of the combined squadrons of France and Spain to the West Indies, and again at the Battle of Trafalgar.

Bayntun's father was a diplomat stationed as Consul-General at Algiers, and it was there that Henry was born in 1766. He entered the Royal Navy at an early age and gained his lieutenancy in 1783. In 1794, Bayntun was with Sir John Jervis in the West Indies and was involved in the capture of Martinique and gained command of the *Avenger* (16) following the death of her captain. With her boats, Bayntun took part in the boarding and capture of the French frigate *Bienvenue* (32) and other shipping in Fort Royal Bay on 17 March 1794. This action was followed by the capture of Guadeloupe in the next month, which resulted in his being promoted commander and then captain over the next few months.

Bayntun then commanded the *Reunion* (36), which was unfortunately wrecked in December 1796. There followed appointments to the *Quebec* frigate, and HMS *Thunderer* (74) and *Cumberland* (74). During this time, Bayntun stayed primarily in the West Indies. With the recommencement of the war in 1803 and in command of the *Cumberland*, Captain Bayntun captured on 30 June the French frigate *Créole* (40) with troops on board and a number of other vessels.

After ten years spent mainly in the West Indies, Bayntun returned to Britain, took command in 1804 of HMS *Leviathan* (74) and joined Nelson in the Mediterranean. In the summer of 1805, he returned briefly to the West Indies during the chase of the Combined Fleet.

At Trafalgar, the *Leviathan* was fourth ship in Nelson's line, following in the wakes of the *Temeraire* and *Neptune*. Both the *Leviathan* and Fremantle's *Neptune* then passed under the stern of the *Bucentaure* and raked her with broadsides. After passing the *Bucentaure*, the *Neptune* moved into position to engage the *Santissima Trinidad*, while Bayntun conned the *Leviathan* toward the French *Neptune* (80), which had been giving Harvey's *Temeraire* much trouble, while Harvey tried to support the *Victory* by engaging the *Redoutable*. The *Neptune* decided not to engage the *Leviathan* and fell off to leeward, so Bayntun turned his attentions toward the massive *Santissima Trinidad*.

About 2.30pm, Bayntun saw Dumanoir's squadron of five ships bearing down on the *Victory*, so he disengaged from the *Santissima Trinidad* and, in company with a number of British ships recently arrived, set course for the French squadron. At about the same time, from the deck of the *Victory*, Hardy saw Dumanoir's squadron approaching and signalled the nearby British ships

---

Date of death: 16 December 1840
Place of death: Bath
Where buried: All Saints Church, Weston, Bath
Description: A stone box tomb in plot 119, north east corner of the graveyard. Headstone and family grave, shared with his wife and two other relatives.
Dimensions: Approx 190 cm x 125 cm

Transcription
———

(part only of inscription on headstone)
Admiral
Sir HENRY WILLIAM BAYNTUN, KCB
Who died the 16 of Dec 1840.
Aged 75

The rest of the inscription concerns his wife Sophia Lady Bayntun, her uncle William Lutwyche, and his wife Mary.

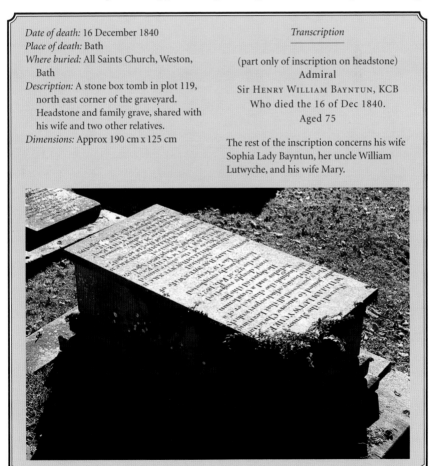

to come to the wind on the larboard tack and block the enemy. The *Leviathan* led this group and found herself on course to attack the Spanish *San Augustin* (74). She then turned out of the line and took position alongside the *San Augustin*, exchanging broadsides at very close quarters. Bayntun then grappled the Spanish ship, called for boarders, and they carried her without much resistance. Unfortunately, the *San Augustin* was one of the prizes burnt during the great storm that followed the battle.

Following Trafalgar, Bayntun took part in Nelson's funeral, carrying the 'guidon' in the splendid processions. He received the naval gold medal and a sword from the Lloyd's Patriotic Fund. In 1807, he took part in the expedition to Buenos Ayres and in 1811, took command of the Royal Yacht *Royal Sovereign*. He advanced through the Navy List, reaching the rank of admiral in 1837 and, having been given the KCB in 1815, was advanced to GCB in 1839. He died at Bath on 16 December 1840.

SCC

Edward Berry
(1768–1831)
Captain HMS *Agamemnon*

Berry was one of Nelson's closest professional friends, and a key member of the original Nile 'Band of Brothers'. As well as serving with Nelson at Cape St Vincent, the Nile and Trafalgar, he took part in six other fleet battles and a large number of smaller actions. A slight, rather delicate man with fair hair and piercing blue eyes, Berry was quick-witted, impulsive and aggressive to the point of recklessness. When he joined the fleet off Cadiz in HMS *Agamemnon*, on 13 October 1805, just prior to Trafalgar, Nelson is supposed to have said, 'Here comes that fool, Berry. *Now* we shall have a fight!'

He was born in 1768, the son of a London merchant. His father died young, leaving his large family with little means of support, and so the boy entered the Navy in 1777 at the very early age of eleven as a midshipman in the *Burford*.

Date of death:
13 February 1831
Place of death: Bath
Where buried:
St Swithin's Church,
Walcot, Bath
Description: Headstone
located against a wall
on the west side of
the church. The
graveyard has been
cleared and the
headstone moved
from its original site.

Photograph and transcription on page 25

WALL PLAQUE, in
marble, on west wall
inside St Swithin's
church, Walcot, Bath.
Description: Coat of
arms above inscription,
with the motto
"AD ALTIORA"

Transcription

SACRED TO THE MEMORY OF

SIR **EDWARD BERRY**, BARONET,

KNIGHT COMMANDER OF THE MOST HONOURABLE AND MILITARY ORDER

OF THE BATH,

AND REAR ADMIRAL OF THE RED SQUADRON OF HIS MAJESTY'S FLEET,

HE DEPARTED THIS LIFE 13TH OF FEBRUARY 1831,

IN THE 63RD YEAR OF HIS AGE.

THE DISTINGUISHED SERVICES OF SIR **EDWARD BERRY**,

ARE RECORDED IN THE ANNALS OF HIS COUNTRY.

HE WAS THE FRIEND AND COMPANION OF **LORD NELSON**, UNDER WHOSE COMMAND

HE FOUGHT AT THE BATTLE OF ST VINCENT, THE NILE, AND TRAFALGAR;

HE COMMANDED H:M:SHIP AGAMEMNON AT THE BATTLE OF ST DOMINGO,

AND WAS HONORED BY HIS SOVEREIGN WITH *THREE* MEDALS,

FOR GREAT NAVAL VICTORIES.

"BE STRONG AND OF GOOD COURAGE, BE NOT AFRAID, NEITHER BE THOU DISMAYED: FOR

THE LORD THY GOD IS WITH THEE WHITHERSOEVER THOU GOEST." Josh.Chap. 1 Ver. 9

ALSO

TO DAME LOUISA HENRIETTA BERRY

HIS WIDOW

BORN 10TH JULY 1779

DIED 7TH MAY 1856

Promoted lieutenant in 1794 for bravery in boarding a French man of war, while serving in the West Indies, his conduct came to the attention of the commander-in-chief, Admiral Sir John Jervis. So when later, in 1796, Commodore Horatio Nelson was looking for a new first lieutenant for his ship HMS *Agamemnon*, Jervis (by then commanding in the Mediterranean) recommended Berry. The two took an instant liking to each other and formed a close partnership. When Nelson transferred to the *Captain* in 1796, Berry went with him.

Jervis continued to support Berry and obtained his promotion to commander in early 1797. But there was no ship ready for him and so he remained in the *Captain* as a passenger. He was thus with Nelson at the Battle of Cape St Vincent (14 February 1797) and fought alongside him in the boarding party that captured two Spanish ships. Running out along the *Captain*'s bowsprit, he led one division onto the poop of the *San Nicolas* while Nelson led another through her stern windows.

In March 1798, Berry was made a post captain and Nelson (at that time in England recovering from the loss of his arm) immediately asked him to be his flag captain in the *Vanguard*. He fought with distinction at the Battle of the Nile (1 August 1798) and it was into his arms that Nelson reeled when he was hit on the forehead by a piece of flying shrapnel, with the words, 'I am killed. Remember me to my wife.' Given the honour of carrying Nelson's dispatches home in HMS *Leander*, Berry was captured by one of the French battleships that had escaped from the Nile, the *Généreux*, and was badly wounded in the arm. He was exchanged and finally reached England in December, where he was knighted and presented with the freedom of the City of London.

He was then given command of the Third Rate battleship *Foudroyant* and sent out in her to the Mediterranean in June 1799, to replace Nelson's battered flagship *Vanguard*. He commanded the *Foudroyant* during the capture of Malta from the French occupying force and also at the capture of his former captor, the *Généreux*, and her fellow-escapee from the Nile, the *Guillaume Tell*.

Nelson left the Mediterranean in the summer of 1800 and Berry took the *Foudroyant* home to England, where he remained until the summer of 1805, when he was appointed to HMS *Agamemnon* and joined Nelson in time for Trafalgar. HMS *Agamemnon* was towards the rear of Nelson's line and so she did not get into action until nearly 2pm. She joined the *Neptune* and *Conqueror* in pounding the mighty four-decked Spanish battleship *Santissima Trinidad* until she was forced to surrender. In the closing stages, when the enemy van, under Dumanoir, threatened an attack on the badly-damaged British ships, HMS *Agamemnon* formed part of the hastily-formed line of battle that drove them away. As the smoke of battle began to clear away, Berry felt a premonition that something was wrong on board the *Victory* and, calling for his boat, he had himself rowed across to the stricken flagship. But he arrived just too late to bid farewell to the dying Nelson.

The following year, Berry, still commanding the *Agamemnon*, took part in

Transcription

WITHIN THIS TOMB
ARE DEPOSITED
THE MORTAL REMAINS OF
SIR EDWARD BERRY
BARONET
KNIGHT COMMANDER
OF THE
MOST HONORABLE AND
MILITARY
ORDER OF THE BATH
AND REAR ADMIRAL OF
THE RED
SQUADRON OF HIS
MAJESTY'S FLEET
HE WAS BORN ON THE
17TH OF APRIL
1768
HE DEPARTED THIS LIFE
ON THE
13TH OF FEBRUARY 1831

ALSO
TO LOUISA HENRIETTA
BERRY
HIS WIDOW BORN 10TH
JULY 1779
DIED 7TH MAY 1856

the Battle of San Domingo (6 February 1806) and was made a baronet. He remained in active service until 1813 when he was placed in command of one of the royal yachts, but his health was broken and, although he became a rear admiral in 1821, he never hoisted his flag. He died in Bath on 13 February 1831 and was buried in the graveyard of Walcot church.

CSW

THE HONOURABLE HENRY BLACKWOOD

(1770–1832)
Captain HMS *Euryalus*

Early on the morning of 2 September 1805, Captain the Honourable Henry Blackwood, of HMS *Euryalus*, arrived at Lymington and took a carriage to London with dispatches from Vice Admiral Collingwood, reporting that the combined French and Spanish fleets had taken refuge in Cadiz. He stopped briefly at Merton to advise Nelson of the news before proceeding on to the Admiralty. When Nelson was put in command of the British fleet and sailed for Cadiz in HMS *Victory*, Blackwood was in attendance in HMS *Euryalus* and went on board the *Victory* a number of times for discussions with Nelson. On arrival, Nelson put Blackwood in charge of the frigates and fast battleships watching the combined fleet, with instructions not to fail to inform him if it should sail, a task which Blackwood performed splendidly. During the battle, HMS *Euryalus* acted as signal frigate to HMS *Victory*, and after Nelson's death, Collingwood shifted his flag to her. Because of his proficiency in French, Blackwood not only had the task of liaising with the Governor of Cadiz over the exchange of wounded sailors, but also the job of carrying the captured Admiral Villeneuve and his suite to England. So Blackwood performed a number of ancillary roles in the great victory of Trafalgar.

Born on 28 December 1769 in Northern Ireland, the seventh son and tenth child of Sir John Blackwood, Henry Blackwood joined the Royal Navy at the age of twelve, and served his time as a midshipman before passing his lieutenant's examination in 1789. His first significant fleet action was in 1794 at the Battle of the Glorious First of June, in which he was the first lieutenant of HMS *Invincible*, and after the battle was given command of the captured *La Juste*, and brought the prize into Portsmouth. He was promoted commander and given command of the fireship HMS *Megaera*. He was made a post captain in June 1795. After time in HMS *Nonsuch*, he was given command of HMS *Brilliant* in which he distinguished himself in a skirmish off the Azores, with two larger French frigates. He then took command of HMS *Penelope* in which his gallantry first came to Nelson's attention. As one of the watching frigates off Malta, the frigate HMS *Penelope* (36) spotted the shadowy form of the French ship *Guillaume Tell* (80) trying to slip away unobserved – Blackwood gave chase, and by superb seamanship managed to damage the much larger French ship and slow her down, until the British ships of the line came up to finish the job. Nelson wrote a very warm letter to Blackwood as a result of his action, beginning,

Is there a sympathy which ties men together in the bonds of friendship without having a personal knowledge of each other? If so (and I believe it was so to you) I was your friend and acquaintance before I saw you.

June 1803 saw Blackwood as the captain of the new frigate HMS *Euryalus*, built at the famous Adams yard at Buckler's Hard, in which he saw much service in the English Channel, watching the French preparations for invasion. Then in 1805 came the Battle of Trafalgar. Blackwood enjoyed Nelson's confidences and friendship – he was even, with Captain Thomas Hardy, a witness to Nelson's

WALL PLAQUE, in white marble against a grey marble background, with two scallops below.
Location: Westminster Abbey, London, north transept, northernmost bay, east side at the top, on the back of the Pitt monument.
Sculptor: W Behnes.
Note: In Westminster Abbey muniments is a letter of 27 May 1833, in which Behnes asks Dean Ireland for the fee that will be required for the monument. He was to receive £300, so that it would 'not be of any considerable magnitude'. Behnes sent a pencil sketch.

Transcription:

SACRED TO THE MEMORY
OF VICE ADMIRAL THE
HONORABLE SIR HENRY
BLACKWOOD, BART.
K.C.B.G.C.

WHO DIED DEC THE 13TH 1832,
AGED SIXTY THREE YEARS, FIFTY ONE OF
WHICH HE HAD SPENT IN THE ACTIVE
SERVICE OF HIS PROFESSION,
DISTINGUISHED BY HIS EARLY
PROMPTITUDE AND BRAVERY, QUALITIES
WHICH DERIVED ADDITIONAL LUSTRE
FROM THE VIRTUES WHICH ADORNED HIS
PERSONAL CHARACTER; WITH VALOUR
COMBINING A STRONG SENSE OF
RELIGION, AND THE ELEVATION OF AN
UPRIGHT NOBLE MIND WITH ALL THE
ENDEARING FEELINGS OF A MANLY
GENEROUS AND BENEVOLENT HEART.

THIS TRIBUTE OF SORROW AND
AFFECTION TO THE MEMORY OF ONE SO
JUSTLY HONORED AND BELOVED IS
OFFERED BY HIS DEEPLY AFFLICTED
WIDOW AND HIS SURVIVING CHILDREN.

Date of death: 13 December 1832
Place of death: Ballyleidy House, Co Down, N Ireland
Where buried: St John the Evangelist Church, Killyleagh, Co Down
Description: Bricked-up vault in the churchyard of St John's Church, Killyleagh. There is a granite arch over the entrance which is believed to have 4-5 steps down inside. It has been filled with soil.

famous last codicil to his will, in which he left Emma Hamilton and their daughter as 'a legacy to my King and Country'.

At Nelson's funeral, Captain Blackwood attended as trainbearer to the chief mourner, Admiral of the Fleet Sir Peter Parker. He was then appointed to command of HMS *Ajax* and sailed to join the Mediterranean fleet, but in the opening stages of the Dardanelles operation, disaster struck and the *Ajax* caught fire, with great loss of life. Blackwood was fully exonerated of blame, and after returning to England was given command of the new HMS *Warspite* (74), and stayed with her, principally in the Mediterranean, for the next five years.

In 1814, he was appointed captain of the fleet to Prince William Henry, Duke of Clarence. In that role, he was responsible for the arrangements for the reception for the Tsar of Russia and the King of Prussia, when they visited Britain following the first defeat of Napoleon, including a fleet review at Spithead. Later that year, he was promoted rear admiral of the blue and was made a baronet, and in 1819 was created a KCB.

At the end of 1819, Sir Henry was appointed Commander-in-Chief East Indies, and sailed in HMS *Leander*, to be based principally at Trincomalee,

WALL MEMORIAL in marble and slate, in the east corner of Killyleagh Church.

Description: Includes a coat of arms below, inscribed 'Tria juncta in uno' and with the motto 'Per vias rectas', and two flags inscribed 'Guillaume Tell', 'Penelope' and 'Trafalgar', 'Euryalus'.

Dimensions: 242 cm x 130 cm.

Sculptor: Not named, but possibly Hastings of Downpatrick.

Transcription

TO THE MEMORY OF
VICE ADMIRAL THE HON SIR HENRY BLACKWOOD, BART.
WHOSE REMAINS ARE DEPOSITED IN THE FAMILY VAULT ADJOINING THIS CHURCH.
HE WAS BORN AT KILLYLEAGH IN THE YEAR 1769, THE SEVENTH SON OF
SIR JOHN BLACKWOOD, BART. AND DORCAS BARONESS DUFFERIN AND CLANEBOYE.
AT THE AGE OF ELEVEN YEARS HE ENTERED THE NAVAL SERVICE, AND BECAME
IN AFTER LIFE ONE OF ITS MOST DISTINGUISHED COMMANDERS.
VALIANT, GENEROUS, AND WARM HEARTED, PROMPT, AND DECIDED IN DANGER,
BUT NEVER RASH, HE OBTAINED THE RESPECT AS WELL AS CONFIDENCE
OF THOSE WITH WHOM HE SERVED, HE REJOICED TO ENCOURAGE MERIT,
AND PROMOTE THE INTERESTS OF THE DESERVING.
BELOVED BY HIS FAMILY, ADMIRED BY ALL, HIS MEMORY WILL LONG BE CHERISHED
IN THE DOMESTIC CIRCLE, AND IN THE ANNALS OF BRITAIN'S NAVAL GLORY
HIS NAME WILL STAND RECORDED WITH THE FOREMOST OF HER HEROES.
HE DIED AT BALLYLEIDY OF TYPHUS FEVER, ON THE 13TH OF DECEMBER 1832.

HE WAS A KNIGHT COMMANDER OF THE ORDER OF THE BATH, AND
A KNIGHT GRAND CROSS OF THE ROYAL HANOVERIEN [SIC] GUELPHIC ORDER.

returning home in December 1822. In 1827, he was appointed Commander-in-Chief Nore, a post that he held until August 1830.

Unfortunately, his son Captain Henry Martin Blackwood contracted typhus, and Sir Henry took him to the ancestral home in Northern Ireland to nurse him. Young Henry survived but Sir Henry caught the disease from his son, and died on 13 December 1832, Vice Admiral of the White, leaving his wife and four children.

LB

CHARLES BULLEN

(1769–1853)
Captain HMS *Britannia*

An officer of great personal courage, Charles Bullen was Lord Northesk's flag captain at Trafalgar and the two men had worked well together over seven or eight years. However, Bullen and Nelson had never served together before 1805 and, typically, Nelson made sure he got to know him in the days before Trafalgar by inviting him to dine.

Born on 10 September 1769 in Newcastle, and having entered the service in 1779, young Bullen progressed through sea training and gained his lieutenancy in 1791. He served as lieutenant on board the *Ramillies* during Lord Howe's victory of the Glorious First of June, 1794. He then joined the *Monmouth* (64), whose captain was Lord Northesk. They were both swept into the maw of the Nore Mutiny of 1797. Northesk was treated with respect and even asked by the mutineers to present their grievances to the King; Bullen, on the other hand, was put on trial by the ship's company, who even went so far as to put a noose around his neck.

Northesk resigned his command in protest when the mutineers' demands were rejected, but Bullen continued as the *Monmouth*'s first lieutenant under a new captain, James Walker. He took part in the Battle of Camperdown on 11 October 1797 when the *Monmouth* fought a brutal battle with the *Alkmaar* and *Delft*, both of which surrendered to her. Marshall recounts, '[The *Delft*] was taken possession of by Lieutenant Bullen, who found her in very shoal water, and so dreadfully cut up, that it was with great difficulty he could get her clear of the shore. She sunk under him, when in tow of the *Veteran*, 64, two days after the action.' Many Dutch and British seamen were lost, but many more were saved under Bullen's direction, as they were picked up by the boats of the *Veteran*. Bullen was lucky to be amongst those rescued. For his bravery and exertions during and after Camperdown, Bullen was promoted commander early in 1798. He took command of HMS *Wasp* in 1801 and served a very

WALL PLAQUE, topped by a winged bull, with a ship's stern, inscribed 'Trafalgar'

Location: St James's Church, Shirley, Southampton (in the Cawte Chapel, at head of south aisle)

Material: White marble, mounted on black slate.

Sculptor: Garrets of Southampton.

Dimensions: Plaque: 86 cm x 68.5 cm
Mounting: 101.5 cm x 86.5 cm

Note: In addition, St James's Church, Shirley holds on its north staircase a large diamond-shaped painted hatchment of Sir Charles Bullen, inscribed 'Trafalgar', 'Tria juncta in uno' and 'A rege et victoria'.

Dimensions: 110 cm square in a frame 152 cm square.

Transcription

SACRED TO THE MEMORY OF
ADMIRAL SIR CHARLES BULLEN
G.C.B.G.C.H.
WHO DEPARTED THIS LIFE JULY 2ND 1853,
AGED 86.
HIS LIFE WAS DEVOTED TO THE SERVICE
OF HIS COUNTRY,
AND HE RECEIVED FROM HIS SOVEREIGN
MANY HONORS
FOR THE ACTIVE PART TAKEN IN THE
GLORIOUS ACTIONS OF LORDS DUNCAN,
HOWE, COLLINGWOOD AND NELSON.
THIS LAST TRIBUTE OF AFFECTION IS
PLACED HERE BY HIS NEPHEW
RICHARD BULLEN

arduous time at Sierra Leone, which accounted for his promotion to captain in 1802 upon his return to England.

Bullen then commanded a district of Sea Fencibles and the flotilla equipped in the Thames and Medway, all in anticipation of imminent invasion in 1804. In April 1804, Northesk, then commanding the *Britannia*, was promoted rear admiral and, having hoisted his flag in his former ship, asked for Bullen as his flag captain. In August 1805, they were detached from the Channel Fleet to join the fleet off Cadiz.

At Trafalgar, the *Britannia* was in Nelson's line, sailing in the wake of HMS *Conqueror*. It appears that she passed through the gap in the line made by the *Victory*, but as the *Britannia* was such a slow sailer, she did not arrive until a long

Date of death: 2 July 1853	*Transcription*
Place of death: Shirley, nr Southampton	
Where buried: St Mary's Church, South Stoneham, nr Southampton	SACRED
Description: Headstones and graves of Sir Charles and Lady Bullen, situated alongside each other about ten feet from the east end of the church.	TO THE MEMORY OF ADMIRAL SIR CHARLES BULLEN
Dimensions: 106 cm x 61.5 cm	[subsequently illegible]
	AGED **86**

time after the *Victory*. Lieutenant Royal Marines Lawrence Halloran, who was on board the *Britannia*, described the moment his ship raked the *Santissima Trinidad* in his journal: '[Our guns] shattered the rich display of sculpture, figures, ornaments and inscriptions with which she was adorned. I never saw so beautiful a ship.'

Following Trafalgar, Bullen received the naval gold medal and a sword from the Lloyd's Patriotic Fund (see illustrations on pages 123 and 124). He rose in rank and responsibility, commanding the frigates *Volontaire* and *Cambrian* in the Mediterranean and off the coast of Spain during 1807–11, and the *Akbar* on the North American station during 1814–17. He was commissioner of Chatham Dockyard and superintendent of Pembroke Dockyard during the 1830s and later captain of the Royal Yacht *Royal Sovereign*. Having been made a CB in 1815, he rose to KCB in 1839 and GCB in 1852. He reached the rank of admiral in 1852 and was the last of the Trafalgar Captains to die – at Shirley in Hampshire on 2 July 1853.

SCC

THE HONOURABLE SIR THOMAS BLADEN CAPEL
(1776–1853)
Captain HMS *Phoebe*

Capel became one of Nelson's protégés in 1798 when he was made signal lieutenant of HMS *Vanguard*, Nelson's flagship at the Battle of the Nile (1798). His ability and aristocratic pedigree caught Nelson's eye and, although junior to many of the *Vanguard*'s other lieutenants, Capel was given the honour of taking a copy of the Nile dispatches to London, firstly as commander of HMS *Mutine* and then overland across Europe. The original dispatches were captured by the French, and so it was Capel who brought the official news of the victory to the Admiralty. This ensured that the Admiralty would approve Nelson's promotion of Capel to commander, and in his remarks to their Lordships Nelson stated that Capel was 'a most excellent officer'.

The youngest son of William, fourth Earl of Essex, Capel was born on 25 August 1776 in Hanover Square, London. In order to gain sea time Capel 'officially' entered the Royal Navy on the books of HMS *Phaeton* in 1782, although he actually joined the Navy in 1792 on board HMS *Assistance* off Newfoundland as captain's servant. He was soon made midshipman of HMS *Syren* and Captain Graham Moore wrote of him that he was 'a remarkable fine young man and one whom I am convinced will turn out a meritorious officer' and when Capel was transferred to another ship that 'I shall regret Capel [leaving].' After serving as a midshipman in a number of ships, he saw his first major fleet action in HMS *Sans Pareil* when Lord Bridport's fleet took three French men-of-war off L'Orient on 23 July 1795. On 16 May 1796, Capel was made acting lieutenant and this promotion was confirmed in April of the following year. After delivering the Nile dispatches, Capel was confirmed in his rank of commander and was shortly after given post rank as captain of HM Sloop *Alecto*.

Capel then started his career as one of the Navy's star frigate captains for the next eight and a half years, particularly distinguishing himself in operations with Spanish irregular forces off the coast of Spain. However, in June 1800, he had the misfortune to run his ship, HMS *Meleager*, onto rocks off the Gulf of Mexico. After burning the ship to stop it falling into Spanish hands, he transferred the crew onto a nearby island where they were subsequently rescued. In 1803, he was appointed to the frigate HMS *Phoebe* and served with Nelson throughout the Mediterranean campaign, becoming one of the admiral's favourite young captains, who was often given special tasks of reconnaissance and information gathering.

When Nelson left the Mediterranean in May 1805 to pursue Villeneuve to the West Indies and back, he left Capel in the Mediterranean, in command of a small squadron of five frigates and two bomb vessels, with orders to cover Sardinia, Sicily and the approaches to Egypt. During the Battle of Trafalgar, as a frigate, the *Phoebe*'s task was to repeat signals and to stand by to assist in any way

Date of death: 4 March 1853
Place of death: 22 Rutland Gate, London (his home)
Where buried: Kensal Green Cemetery, London (Plot 10680/77/IR)
Description: Plot granted 8 March 1853 for 15 guineas to Dame Harriet Capel (widow). A brick grave set in mortar, capable of taking 6 coffins (Dame Harriet was buried there in 1866). Sir Thomas' tomb is the centre of three Capel family tombs, to the left being that of an unknown member of the family, and to the right that of Lady Caroline Capel. Each tomb consists of a brick vault, overlaid by a main limestone slab 25 cm thick, under which an underslab 10 cm thick is visible. On the top of the main slab there is an upper slab which carries the main inscriptions. Sir Thomas' tomb is ridged with sloping faces like a pitched roof.

Sir Thomas' main inscription is readable except for two dates. There is also an inscription running round the upper slab, which is mostly illegible. Lady Caroline's inscription is legible, but not the one on the third grave (the 'unknown' member of the family).

Dimensions: Each grave is 122 cm x 274 cm overall, with 2 cm between them.

Transcription

IN MEMORY OF
ADMIRAL THE HONORABLE
SIR THOMAS BLADEN CAPEL
WHO DEPARTED THIS LIFE ON
[*ILLEGIBLE DATE*]
THUS CLOSING A LONG AND
DISTINGUISHED CAREER OF
SERVICE RENDERED TO HIS
COUNTRY DURING WHICH TIME
HE SERVED ACTIVELY FOR
THIRTY ONE YEARS
FROM HIS ENTRY INTO THE ROYAL
NAVY IN [*DATE*] UNTIL HIS DEATH
NILE
DARDANELLES
TRAFALGAR

There is also a mostly illegible inscription running round all four sides of the upper slab

that she could and took no part in the fighting. During the gale that followed the battle, the *Phoebe* 'by extraordinary exertions' helped save the French prize *Swiftsure* (not to be confused with the British ship of the same name) from destruction.

Following the Trafalgar campaign, Capel was made captain of the man-of-war HMS *La Hogue* in 1811 and commanded a small squadron of ships blockading US frigates off the coast of New London during the War of 1812. At the end of the war, Capel commanded one of the royal yachts, became rear admiral in 1825 and hoisted his flag as commander in chief of the East India station from 1834 to 1837. He was made KCB in 1832 and GCB in 1852. Towards the end of his life, he sat on the committee that organised the issue of the Naval General Service Medal, which included a clasp for Trafalgar. He died in London on 4 March 1853.

NS

EDWARD CODRINGTON

(1770–1851)

Captain HMS *Orion*

Edward Codrington had never served with Nelson before September 1805 and yet he quickly became an admirer. Moreover, he showed by his actions at Trafalgar that he both understood, and fully supported, Nelson's battle plan and style of fighting. Alone of all the Trafalgar captains, he later commanded a British fleet in battle, at Navarino in 1827.

The son of a landowner and grandson of a baronet, he was born on 27 April 1770 and educated at Harrow before joining the Royal Navy in 1783. He became a lieutenant in 1793 and was signal officer of Admiral Lord Howe's flagship, HMS *Queen Charlotte*, at the Glorious First of June in 1794. A personal protégé of Howe, he was given the honour of taking home the admiral's duplicate dispatches and, as was customary, was rewarded with promotion to the rank of commander. The following year he was made a captain and was present, in command of the frigate *La Babet*, at Bridport's action off Groix on 23 June.

He remained in frigates until May 1805, when he was appointed to command the battleship HMS *Orion* (74) and, after a short spell with the Channel Fleet, was detached to reinforce Collingwood off Cadiz. He found Collingwood's rather dour regime uncongenial and was delighted when Nelson was

WALL PLAQUE
Location: St Mary's Church, Dodington Park, S Glos. Set on right side of entrance above an interior door.
Description: Rectangular wall plaque, white marble mounted on black slate.
Dimensions: Plaque: 152 cm x 92 cm
Slate: 175 cm x 118 cm
Note: Dodington Park Estate used to be owned by the Codrington family until it was sold recently to Mr James Dyson. There is no public access
Transcription overleaf.

Date of death: 28 April 1851
Place of death: Eaton Square, London
Where buried: St Peter's Church, Eaton Square, London
Note: Buried in the crypt of St Peter's Church. At the end of 1952 or early 1953 the church needed to clear the crypt for use as a parish hall. Part of it had been bricked up, and Sir Edward's coffin was found among four hundred coffins there. All the remains were removed to Brookwood Cemetery, Surrey, by night. According to one unconfirmed report, they were re-interred in Plot 70 at Brookwood, but a ground search shows nothing visible there. There was a memorial tablet in St Peter's Church until it was destroyed in a disastrous fire in 1987. According to the Church History, this tablet recorded that Sir Edward 'captained the Orion at Trafalgar and commanded the combined British, French and Russian fleet at Navarino in 1827. His family long took a leading part in the affairs of St Peter's…his great-grandson Colonel Sir Geoffrey Codrington (1888-1973) caused the inscription about his great-grand father's coffin to be cut.' Unfortunately the church no longer has a transcript of this inscription.

appointed to command the fleet. At their first meeting, Nelson bound the young captain to him with one of his characteristic gestures – he handed Codrington a letter from his wife saying that 'being entrusted with it by a lady, he made a point of delivering it himself.'

At Trafalgar, the *Orion* was towards the rear of Nelson's line and so did not arrive in the thick of the fighting until about two hours after the first shot was fired. Codrington planned his approach carefully, holding his fire so as not to obscure his view with smoke, and even when he reached the action, he passed through the clusters of ships until he came across a suitable victim. She was the French *Swiftsure* into whose stern the *Orion*'s gunners poured a series of murderous broadsides, forcing her to surrender. Codrington then attempted to take on the *Principe de Asturias*, flagship of the Spanish commander-in-chief, Don Frederico Gravina, but she pulled away, so he moved on northwards to assist the British ships there in repelling the attack by Dumanoir and the French van. The *Orion* then played a key role in the capture of the gallantly-defended *L'Intrepide*, sailing right round the stricken ship pouring in a deadly, accurate fire from close quarters. It was a classic demonstration of the sort of mobile, intelligent fighting that Nelson wanted. Like the other captains, Codrington was rewarded with the naval gold medal and a sword from the Lloyd's Patriotic Fund.

Having remained with Collingwood in the Mediterranean until December 1806, Codrington eventually returned home. He continued in active service throughout the rest of the war, serving in the disastrous amphibious attack on the Dutch island of Walcheren in 1809 and off the coast of Spain, commanding a squadron supporting Wellington's land campaign, during 1811–13. Promoted rear admiral in 1814, he was captain of the fleet to the commander-in-chief of the North American station, Sir Alexander Cochrane, during the closing stages of the war with America, and took part in operations in the Chesapeake River and in the attack on New Orleans.

In 1826, by then a vice admiral, he became commander in chief in the Mediterranean, with his flag flying in HMS *Asia*. At that time, the Greeks were in open revolt against their Turkish overlords. Britain, although not formally at war with Turkey, was generally sympathetic to the Greek cause, which placed Codrington in a difficult position politically. The growing tension eventually led to a full-scale battle in the Bay of Navarino in southern Greece, on 20 October 1827, where the Turkish fleet was annihilated by a combined British, French and Russian fleet under Codrington's command, thus paving the way for Greek independence, which came two years later. It was the last major naval battle fought wholly under sail.

Although the victory was popular with the people of Britain, the government was embarrassed by such overt intervention and recalled Codrington 'for explanations'. However, he was cleared of blame and received the Grand Cross of the Bath. He continued to serve in the Navy, commanding the Channel squadron in 1831/2 and ending a long and distinguished career as commander in chief at Plymouth during 1839–42. He lived long enough to

MEMORIAL TABLET

Location: Crypt of St Paul's Cathedral, London

Description: A marble wall plaque, with a left profile of Codrington surmounted by a naval crown, with flags and the word 'Navarin'. Below is an embossed coat of arms of Codrington.

Sculptor: Albert Bruce Joy (it is believed that Joy is responsible only for the portrait profile of Codrington)

Dimensions:
162 x 117cm

Transcription

IN MEMORY OF
ADMIRAL SIR EDWARD CODRINGTON, G.C.B.,
BORN 27TH OF APRIL 1770, DIED 28TH OF APRIL 1851.

HE ENTERED THE NAVY 1783; WAS LIEUTENANT OF H.M.S. 'QUEEN CHARLOTTE'
IN THE BATTLE OF THE 1ST OF JUNE 1794;
COMMANDER IN THE ACTION OF THE 23RD JUNE 1795;
CAPTAIN OF H.M.S. 'ORION' IN THE BATTLE OF TRAFALGAR 21ST OCTOBER 1805;
CAPTAIN OF H.M.S. 'BLAKE' IN THE SCHELDT, AND ON THE EAST COAST OF SPAIN 1809-13;
SERVED ON THE COAST OF N. AMERICA 1814.
HE WAS COMMANDER-IN-CHIEF OF THE ALLIED FLEETS OF ENGLAND, FRANCE, AND RUSSIA,
IN THE BATTLE OF NAVARIN, 20TH OCTOBER 1827.

claim the Naval General Service Medal with four clasps in 1848 and eventually died at his home in Eaton Square, London, in 1851. He was buried in St Peter's, Eaton Square, but when the crypt was cleared in 1953, the body was moved with others to Brookwood Cemetery and its exact whereabouts are now unknown. He is, however, memorialised in St Paul's Cathedral, his own church of St Mary's, Dodington, and, most appropriately, at Pylos in Greece.

CSW

CUTHBERT, LORD COLLINGWOOD
(1748–1810)
Vice Admiral and second-in-command HMS *Royal Sovereign*

'See how that noble fellow Collingwood takes his ship into action!' remarked Nelson to Captain Henry Blackwood. The *Royal Sovereign* leading the Lee Division was bearing down on the rear of the Combined Fleet, engaging the enemy at least fifteen minutes before any other British ship. As a midshipman observing him more closely recollected, 'I see before me dear old Cuddie (as we called Collingwood) walking the break of the poop, with his little triangular gold-laced cocked hat, tight silk stockings, and buckles, musing over the progress of the fight and munching an apple.' Collingwood was enjoying himself. 'Oh Rotheram', he exclaimed to the *Royal Sovereign*'s captain, 'what would Nelson give to be here!' According to Blackwood, 'he fought like an Angel.'

The *Royal Sovereign* had a severe duel with the Spanish *Santa Ana* and sustained much damage to her masts and rigging. When the news came that Nelson was mortally wounded, Collingwood realised that he would have to take command and signalled Blackwood in the *Euryalus* to come and take the helpless hull of his flagship in tow. The 'butcher's bill' listed 141 officers and crew killed and wounded. Collingwood was among them, although he did not allow his name to be included on the list. 'Did I not tell you how my leg was hurt?' he later wrote to his wife. 'It was by a splinter – a pretty severe blow.' Collingwood had married the daughter of Newcastle's Lord Mayor in 1791.

Of the fifteen ships in Collingwood's division at Trafalgar, only six remained in fighting trim. The rest had suffered serious damage. Most were wholly or partially dismasted. Yet, after the battle, Collingwood seems to have forgotten, or even deliberately ignored, Nelson's signal to anchor the fleet 'at the close of day'. While he eventually gave the order at 9pm, he was more concerned to write his now-famous dispatch, which begins, 'The ever-to-be-lamented death of Vice Admiral Lord Viscount Nelson, who, in the late conflict with the enemy, fell in the hour of victory, leaves to me the duty of informing my Lords Commissioners of the Admiralty…'; and includes the poignant phrase, 'My heart is rent with the most poignant grief for the death of a friend, to whom, by many years intimacy…I was bound by the strongest ties of affection.'

After Trafalgar, Collingwood was awarded a pension of £2,000, a baronetcy and the naval gold medal (see illustrations on page 124). He was also promoted vice admiral of the red, but he did not return to England.

Cuthbert Collingwood was born in 1748 at Morpeth, near Newcastle-upon-Tyne. His father was an unsuccessful merchant. He entered the Navy as a

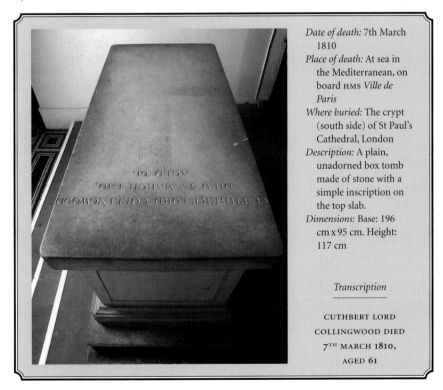

Date of death: 7th March 1810

Place of death: At sea in the Mediterranean, on board HMS *Ville de Paris*

Where buried: The crypt (south side) of St Paul's Cathedral, London

Description: A plain, unadorned box tomb made of stone with a simple inscription on the top slab.

Dimensions: Base: 196 cm x 95 cm. Height: 117 cm

Transcription

CUTHBERT LORD
COLLINGWOOD DIED
7TH MARCH 1810,
AGED 61

MEMORIAL

Location: South transept, St Paul's Cathedral, London

Description: Made in 1813 of marble, Collingwood's body, partially wrapped in a shroud, and holding his sword, rests on a funeral barge with a prow carved to look like the bow of a line-of-battle ship. He is mourned by two figures – on the left, an angel supporting his head, and on the right by Neptune, supported by two cherubs.

Sculptor: Richard Westmacott

Transcription

ERECTED AT THE PUBLIC EXPENSE TO THE MEMORY OF

CUTHBERT, LORD COLLINGWOOD,

WHO DIED IN THE COMMAND OF THE FLEET IN THE MEDITERRANEAN, ON BOARD OF

THE VILLE-DE-PARIS,

VII. MARCH MDCCCX. IN THE LXI YEAR OF HIS AGE.

WHEREVER HE SERVED HE WAS DISTINGUISHED FOR CONDUCT, SKILL, AND COURAGE;

PARTICULARLY IN THE ACTION WITH THE FRENCH FLEET, 1. JUNE MDCCXCIV, AS

CAPTAIN OF THE BARFLEUR;

IN THE ACTION WITH THE SPANISH FLEET, XIV. FEBRUARY MDCCXVII.

AS CAPTAIN OF THE EXCELLENT; BUT MOST CONSPICUOUSLY IN THE DECISIVE VICTORY

OFF CAPE TRAFALGAR, OBTAINED OVER

THE COMBINED FLEETS OF FRANCE AND SPAIN:

TO WHICH HE EMINENTLY CONTRIBUTED, AS VICE-ADMIRAL OF THE BLUE,

COMMANDING THE LARBOARD DIVISION,

XXI. OCTOBER MDCCCV.

volunteer under the patronage of Admiral Braithwaite and was posted to the frigate *Shannon* in 1761. His early career was spent on the North American station and he was at the abortive British attack on Bunker's Hill, Boston, in 1775. Acquitted by court martial for disobedience of orders, he made captain in 1780, and took command of the *Hinchingbroke* in succession to Horatio Nelson, and thereafter his career closely shadowed that of his friend. They served together on the West Indies station in the mid-1780s and they commanded ships at the Battle of Cape St Vincent in 1797, Collingwood in HMS *Excellent*. Finally, they both led the British to victory at Trafalgar.

There were many similarities between the two men, but Collingwood lacked Nelson's vision, sense of greatness, psychological awareness and predatory instincts. He carefully executed Nelson's orders at Trafalgar. He did not contribute to them. As he remarked on seeing Nelson's signal, 'England expects that every man will do his duty', 'I wish Nelson would stop signalling. We all know what we have to do.'

Captain George Duff described him as 'a fine, steady good officer', and Nelson, talking to Captain Locker, exclaimed, 'What an amiable good man he is! All the rest are geese.' Collingwood was undoubtedly intelligent, articulate and cultivated. He had a dry sense of humour, although some thought him dour. However, his strong sense of public duty required a self-denial and stoicism that many fellow officers found stern and hard to emulate. Nonetheless, he was a good seaman and was loved by those in his own ship for his humanity, compassion, fair-mindedness and reluctance to flog. Unlike Nelson, he was not able to project these feelings to the fleet as a whole. Moreover, he found decision-making difficult, a weakness compounded by his poor ability to delegate and a fascination with minutiae. He was described by one contemporary as 'a selfish old bear...with few, if any friends and no

FAMILY HOME
Location: Morpeth
Description: House, marked by a plaque above the front door.

Transcription

HERE LIVED THE FAMILY OF
VICE ADMIRAL LORD COLLINGWOOD

AND HERE HE SPENT THE FEW AND SHORT
PERIODS OF REPOSE SNATCHED FROM LONG
AND ARDUOUS SERVICE AFLOAT

"WHENEVER I THINK HOW I AM TO BE HAPPY AGAIN
MY THOUGHTS CARRY ME BACK TO MORPETH"
COLLINGWOOD

"SEE HOW THAT NOBLE FELLOW COLLINGWOOD
TAKES HIS SHIP INTO ACTION." NELSON AT TRAFALGAR

ERECTED BY THE CORPORATION OF MORPETH
1905

THE TRAFALGAR CAPTAINS

admirers. In body and mind he was iron and very cold iron.'

It is wretched that this honest and sentimental man not only lost his closest friend, Nelson, but also never returned to England to see his wife and daughter, or his beloved garden in Northumberland. He had to endure a further five years of oceanic seclusion trying to hold down the French in the Mediterranean, and died four days after his orders to return to England reached him on 3 March 1810. His body was brought to England and, like Nelson's, lay in state in the Painted Hall at Greenwich, before being buried in the crypt of St Paul's Cathedral by the side of his dear and close friend. Few men have risen to such eminence while being so long out of the public eye.

PW

BUST AND MEMORIAL

Location: At west end of Newcastle-upon-Tyne Cathedral

Description: A white marble draped cenotaph with, above, a shield and sword and inscription 'Trafalgar' and 'Ferar unus et idem'. A bust of the deceased on pedestal, with four ships carved on each side behind two columns each with four ships' sterns. On a stone plinth simulating rock in sea.

Dimensions: Base 238 cm x 100cm.
Inscription 86 cm x 52 cm.
Overall height 380 cm.

Architect: R Cockerell, London

Sculptor: C Rossi RA, London

Transcription

1ST OF JUNE.   ST VINCENTS.   TRAFALGAR.

SACRED TO THE MEMORY OF

THE RIGHT HONORABLE CUTHBERT BARON COLLINGWOOD,

VICE ADMIRAL OF THE RED AND MAJOR GENERAL OF MARINES, WHO WAS BORN IN THIS TOWN OF
AN ANCIENT FAMILY. HE SERVED WITH GREAT BRAVERY IN THE ACTION OF THE 1ST OF JUNE 1794,
AND BORE A MOST DISTINGUISHED PART IN THE VICTORY OFF CAPE ST VINCENTS IN 1797.
IN THE MEMORABLE BATTLE OF TRAFALGAR, HE LED THE BRITISH SQUADRONS INTO ACTION,
AND PRESSED FORWARD WITH HIS SINGLE SHIP INTO THE MIDST OF THE
COMBINED FLEETS OF FRANCE AND SPAIN.
ON THAT DAY AFTER THE DEATH OF HIS ILLUSTRIOUS COMMANDER AND FRIEND LORD NELSON,
HE COMPLETED THE MOST GLORIOUS AND DECISIVE VICTORY
THAT IS RECORDED IN THE NAVAL ANNALS OF THE WORLD.
HE HELD THE COMMAND OF THE MEDITERRANEAN FOR NEARLY FIVE YEARS, DURING WHICH HE
NEVER QUITTED HIS VESSEL FOR A SINGLE DAY DISPLAYING UNRIVALLED PROFESSIONAL SKILL, AND
CONDUCTING MANY DIFFICULT AND IMPORTANT NEGOCIATIONS
WITH GREAT POLITICAL SAGACITY AND ADDRESS.
AT LENGTH ON THE DECLINE OF HIS HEALTH HE BECAME ANXIOUS TO REVISIT HIS NATIVE LAND
BUT HAVING LEARNED THAT HIS SERVICES COULD ILL BE SPARED IN THOSE CRITICAL TIMES,
HE REPLIED THAT HIS LIFE WAS HIS COUNTRY'S AND PERSEVERED IN THE DISCHARGE OF HIS
ARDUOUS DUTIES TILL WORN OUT WITH FATIGUE HE EXPIRED AT SEA,
ON THE 7TH OF MARCH 1810, IN THE 61ST YEAR OF HIS AGE.
IN PRIVATE LIFE HE WAS GENEROUS AND AFFECTIONATE, A PIOUS JUST AND EXEMPLARY MAN.
A MONUMENT HAS BEEN RAISED BY PARLIAMENT TO HIS MEMORY IN THE CATHEDRAL CHURCH OF
ST PAULS, WHERE HE LIES BY THE SIDE OF THE HERO, TO WHOM HE SO WORTHILY
SUCCEEDED IN THE BATTLE OF TRAFALGAR.
HIS WIDOW, SARAH, DAUGHTER OF JOHN ERASMUS BLACKETT ESQUIRE, OF THIS TOWN,
AND HIS TWO DAUGHTERS, HAD CAUSED THIS CENOTAPH TO BE CONSTRUCTED,
AND AFTER HER DEATH ON THE 16TH OF SEPTEMBER 1819,
IT WAS INSCRIBED TO BOTH THEIR REVERED AND LAMENTED PARENTS
BY THEIR GRATEFUL CHILDREN

NOTES: Every year, the Cathedral holds a service in memory of Lord Collingwood. There is also a children's event at Christmas which involves various parts of the Cathedral, including the Collingwood memorial.

JOHN CONN
(1764–1810)
Captain HMS *Dreadnought*

Conn was one of Nelson's close professional colleagues, having served with him at the Battle of Copenhagen (2 April 1801) and the attack on Boulogne (15/16 August 1801) before also serving for two years as a captain in his Mediterranean fleet (1803–5). In March 1805, Nelson himself wrote, 'A better or more zealous officer than Captain Conn is not in His Majesty's Service.' Later that year, Conn had the distinction of commanding briefly HMS *Victory* (Nelson's flagship), HMS *Royal Sovereign* (Collingwood's flagship) and then, on 21 October at Trafalgar itself, HMS *Dreadnought*, a sister-ship of the more famous *Temeraire*, launched in 1801.

Conn's family were from Waterford in Ireland but he was baptised at Stoke Damerel in Devon in August 1764. He entered the Navy in February 1778 as a thirteen-year-old volunteer, joining his father, a warrant officer (the gunner), in HMS *Weazle*. He became midshipman and master's mate in HMS *Arrogant* in which he participated at the Battle of the Saintes (12 April 1782) when Admiral Sir George Rodney broke through the French line. He passed as lieutenant in June 1788 but had to wait until the war with France before receiving his first commission in June 1793. In the meantime, he married Margaret Nelson, daughter of the Revd Isaac Nelson, at Stoke Damerel in January 1792.

Conn participated as lieutenant in HMS *Royal Sovereign* in Admiral Lord Howe's victory at the Glorious First of June in 1794, and in HMS *Foudroyant* in Commodore Sir John Borlase Warren's defeat of a French squadron off Donegal on 12 October 1798. He was promoted master and commander in August 1800 and appointed to the command of the *Discovery*, one of the bomb vessels engaged during Nelson's victory over the Danes at the Battle of Copenhagen on 2 April 1801. He subsequently commanded a division of howitzer boats in Nelson's disastrous attack on the French flotilla in Boulogne on the night of 15/16 August 1801. In April 1802, he was made post captain and later took command of HMS *Culloden* accompanied by his son, Henry, a first-class volunteer at the tender age of nine.

In April 1803, he became captain of HMS *Canopus* and spent two years with Nelson in the Mediterranean. Returning to England in the summer of 1805, he became acting captain of HMS *Victory* while Nelson and Hardy were on leave, and was then ordered to take the *Victory* out to Admiral Cornwallis's Channel fleet. The Admiralty countermanded this order after learning that the combined Franco-Spanish fleet had arrived in Cadiz, and Conn was instead ordered to take the newly-refitted HMS *Royal Sovereign* out to the Mediterranean Fleet where Nelson's second-in-command, Admiral Collingwood, would exchange it for his flagship, HMS *Dreadnought*. On 10 October, having arrived with the fleet, Conn exchanged ships, taking over the *Dreadnought* in time to participate as her captain at Trafalgar.

The *Dreadnought*, which was in Collingwood's line, entered the battle at about the time Nelson received his fatal wound. She engaged the *San Juan Nepomuceno*, which was bearing down on the crippled *Bellerophon*, and attacked with such devastating effect that within about fifteen minutes the Spanish ship had surrendered. Conn organised a prize party to board her and then pursued the *Principe de Asturias*, flagship of the Spanish commander in chief, Teniente General Don Frederico Gravina. Although Gravina received a wound in the subsequent fighting from which he later died of blood poisoning, his ship was too quick for the *Dreadnought* and managed to sail away, thus ending Conn's participation in the battle.

Conn remained captain of the *Dreadnought* until June 1806 and subsequently commanded the *San Josef* and the *Hibernia* before taking up what turned out to be his final command, HMS *Swiftsure*. While giving chase in that ship off the Bermuda Islands on 4 May 1810, he fell overboard and, although boats were lowered and the utmost endeavours made to save him, these were unfortunately without effect and he was drowned. This was reported to the Admiralty by Admiral Sir John Borlase Warren, who expressed much regret at the loss of 'so deserving an officer as Captain Conn.'

JG

JOHN COOKE
(1763–1805)
Captain HMS *Bellerophon*

The daredevil Captain John Cooke joined the blockade off Cadiz in the *Bellerophon* on 10 June 1805. Four months later, on the evening of 19 October, he was looking forward to dining with Nelson in the *Victory* when the signal that the enemy were 'coming out of port' changed everything.

At Trafalgar, the order of sailing placed his ship fifth in line of Collingwood's division. Foreseeing the bloodiness of the ensuing battle, he felt that he could be 'bowl'd out' at any time, and in an act of leadership worthy of Nelson took his first lieutenant, William Pryce Cumby, and the master, Edward Overton, into his confidence. He showed them Nelson's memorandum so they knew clearly what they were expected to do. Also, when he made out the admiral's signal, 'England expects that every man will do his duty', Cooke went below to pass it on to the gun crews.

After the *Bellerophon* had broken through the enemy line, the fighting became furious and men were falling all around Cooke as he stood with Cumby and Overton on the quarterdeck. He was locked in combat with the French ship *L'Aigle*, whose captain had

Date of death:
21 October 1805
Place of death:
Trafalgar
Where buried: At sea,
off Cape Trafalgar
WALL PLAQUE
Location: The crypt
of St Paul's
Cathedral, London
Description: A marble
wall plaque in bas
relief. A mourning
Britannia is
supported by two
cherubs, the one
on the left holding
her trident, and
the one on the
right trying on her
helmet. In the
background is the
bow of a two-
decked battleship.
Dimensions: 350
cm x 270 cm

ERECTED AT THE PVBLIC EXPENSE TO THE MEMORY OF CAPTAIN JOHN COOKE, WHO WAS KILLED COMMANDING THE BELLEROPHON, IN THE BATTLE OF TRAFALGAR, IN THE 44TH YEAR OF HIS AGE, AND THE 30TH OF HIS SERVICE

Transcription

ERECTED AT THE PVBLIC EXPENSE TO THE
MEMORY OF CAPTAIN JOHN COOKE, WHO WAS
KILLED COMMANDING THE BELLEROPHON, IN THE
BATTLE OF TRAFALGAR, IN THE 44TH YEAR OF
HIS AGE, AND THE 30TH OF HIS SERVICE

filled her fighting tops and rigging with sharpshooters. Cumby pointed out to his senior that he was wearing his epaulettes, which marked him out to the enemy musketeers in the tops and rigging. Unperturbed, Cooke exclaimed, 'It is too late to take them off. I see my situation, but I will die like a man.' He continued discharging his pistols at the enemy, even killing a French officer on his own quarterdeck. After a short time, he directed Cumby to go down to the gun decks to ensure that the starboard guns kept firing at all costs. Even before Cumby got back to the quarterdeck, he was met by the quartermaster, who had come to inform him that Cooke was very badly wounded, hit twice in the chest by musket balls while reloading his pistols. When Cumby reached the quarterdeck, Cooke was dead. His last words were, 'Let me lie quietly one minute. Tell Lieutenant Cumby never to strike!'

He had been hit at almost the same time as Nelson.

John Cooke was born in 1763. His father, Francis Cooke, was an Admiralty cashier. Aged thirteen, he entered the service as a midshipman in 1776 and saw action almost immediately. His ship, the *Eagle*, was at the attack on Rhode Island during the War of American Independence. Three years later, he was promoted lieutenant and served in the *Duke* at Lord Rodney's victory over De Grasse's French fleet at the Battle of the Saintes, in April 1782. Ten years later, he was promoted commander, served under Admiral Lord Howe, and was in command of the fireship *Incendiary* at another major fleet action at the Glorious First of June in 1794.

Cooke was promoted captain after the battle and appointed captain of the *Nymphe* in 1796, in which he took part in the capture of the French frigates *Resistance* and *Constance* in 1797. Later in the same year, he was at the Nore when the ships there mutinied and his crew put him ashore. Two years later, and now in command of the *Amethyst* (38), he took HRH the Duke of York to Holland for his ill-fated expedition, immortalised by the famous nursery rhyme. He was still in the *Amethyst* when he joined the operations under Lord Bridport, near Quiberon, and in 1800 the expedition to Ferrol under Rear Admiral Sir J B Warren. Close to the end of the French Revolutionary War in 1801, Cooke was in the Channel where he met and captured the French frigate *La Dédaigneuse*, and the Spanish *Général Brune*.

In April 1805, he took command of one of the Navy's oldest ships, the *Bellerophon* (74), affectionately known to her crew as the *Billy Ruffian*. Cooke would have seen her at the Glorious First of June and she was also a veteran of the Battle of the Nile. By now Cooke had a reputation as an excellent officer but a strict disciplinarian. Midshipman John Franklin, later to become the ill-fated arctic explorer, found him 'very gentlemanly and active. I like his appearance much.'

Cooke left behind a wife and an eight-year-old daughter. His widow received the naval gold medal for the battle, and a silver vase from the Lloyd's Patriotic Fund.

PW

WALL PLAQUE

Location: St Andrew's
  Church, Donhead St
  Andrew, Wilts,
  On right hand side of
  entrance.

Material: White marble,
  mounted on black slate.

Dimensions: Marble: 122
  cm x 86 cm
  Slate: 148 cm x 107 cm.

Transcription

SACRED to the Memory of
JOHN COOKE, Esq:r late Captain of
His Majestys ship, BELLEROPHON,
Who, in the Battle
Of TRAFALGAR,
On the 21st of Oct:r *1805*
Having evinced the most consummate skill, And Bravery,
In the conflict of that eventful day, Fell,
In a moment, glorious indeed to his COUNTRY,
But marked by the individual tears Of all who knew him. His inconsolable widow,
Places this tablet to record His virtues and His Fate, Near the spot which he had
chosen As his favourite retirement,
And to which, Having left it at the call of his Country,
He returned no more.
Periit Anno Aetatis 43.

Be merciful to her O God who bends,
And mourns the best of Husbands, Fathers, Friends.
Oh "when she wakes at midnight" but to shed,
Fresh tears of anguish on her lonely bed,
"Thinking on Him who IS NOT," then restrain
Her bitter thoughts and her sad heart sustain.
FATHER OF MERCYS she remembers still
Thy chast'ning hand, and to thy Sov'reign will
Bows silent, but not HOPELESS whilst her eye,
She raises to a bright FUTURITY,
And trusts in better worlds thou wilt restore,
The Happiness she here can meet no more.

LOUISA, Relict of the above
Departed this life at Cheltenham Feby 5th 1853,
Aged 96 Years.

WILLIAM PRYCE CUMBY

(?–1837)
First Lieutenant HMS *Bellerophon*

'Tell Lieutenant Cumby never to strike.' These dying words from his captain at Trafalgar placed an immense and sudden responsibility on the young Lieutenant Cumby's shoulders. He rose to the occasion, survived the battle and served in the Royal Navy until he died.

William Pryce Cumby had followed his father's footsteps into the Royal Navy and was promoted lieutenant in 1793 at the very start of the twenty-two-year-long French Revolutionary and Napoleonic Wars. He was first lieutenant aboard the *Bellerophon* (74), which sailed in Vice Admiral Collingwood's Lee Division at Trafalgar. After breaking the line of the Combined Fleet astern of the

Date of death: 27 September 1837
Place of death: Pembroke Dock
Where buried: Park St, Pembroke Dock
Description: A photograph exists of the original grave in the graveyard of the Dockyard which was cleared by the Council in the 1970s to form a car park. The site is now marked by a simple plaque fixed to a stone backing.
Dimensions: Plaque: 53 cm x 30 cm. Stone surround: 90 cm high x 53 cm wide x 35 cm deep.

Transcription

HERE LIE THE MORTAL REMAINS OF
CAPTAIN WILLIAM PRYCE CUMBY R.N. CB. OF H.M.YACHT
ROYAL SOVEREIGN AND CAPTAIN SUPERINTENDENT OF PEMBROKE
DOCKYARD. AN OFFICER WHOSE ZEAL AND PROFESSIONAL SERVICES
AT TRAFALGAR AND ST.DOMINGO DESERVED AND RECEIVED
THE APPROBATION OF HIS COUNTRY. HIS ACTIVE KINDNESS
IN PROMOTING THE WELFARE OF OTHERS PROCURED HIM
THE AFFECTIONATE REGARD OF ALL WHO KNEW HIM.

THE LOSS OF ONE SO KIND AND GOOD HAS TAUGHT HIS
RELATIONS AND FRIENDS HOW VAIN IS EVERY CONSOLATION
BUT THAT AFFORDED BY RELIGION, BY CHRISTIAN
SUBMISSION, BY CHRISTIAN HOPE.

BORN XXTH MARCH MDCCLXXI
DIED XXVIITH SEPTEMBER MDCCCXXXVII

WALL PLAQUE

Location: St Michael's Church, Heighington, Co Durham, on the north wall of the chancel.

Description: Made of white marble mounted on black marble, the text is surmounted by a relief consisting of cannons, cannon balls, an anchor, a flag, a powder cask, an axe and other naval objects. The base is supported by two brackets and between these is a carved coat of arms with the motto 'VIRTUTE ET OPERA'.

Sculptor: I Ternouth, Pimlico, London

Dimensions: Plaque: 91.5 cm x 81.5 cm
  Backing: 240 cm x 127 cm

Note: Trafalgar House in Heighington, built by Cumby in 1830, still stands in the village, though it is no longer owned by his family.

Transcription

SACRED TO THE MEMORY OF

CAPTAIN WILLIAM PRYCE CUMBY, R.N._C.B.

WHO DIED AT PEMBROKE

CAPTAIN SUPERINTENDENT OF THE NAVAL ARSENAL,

AND IN COMMAND OF THE ROYAL SOVEREIGN YACHT,

XXVII SEPTEMBER MDCCCXXXVII AGED LXVI.

IN THE BATTLE OF TRAFALGAR

WHERE AT AN EARLY PERIOD OF THE ENGAGEMENT HE SUCCEEDED TO THE COMMAND OF THE BELLEROPHON OF 74 GUNS, WHICH WAS THEN OPPOSED IN THE HOTTEST OF THE ACTION TO A SUPERIOR FORCE BEING IN CONTACT WITH THE FRENCH SHIP L'AIGLE, CLOSELY ENGAGED WITH THE SPANISH SHIP EL MONARCA, AND EXPOSED TO THE FIRE OF SEVERAL OTHER SHIPS OF THE ENEMY'S LINE HE NOBLY MAINTAINED THE UNEQUAL CONTEST, DISPLAYING IN THIS CRITICAL POSITION A SKILL AND VALOUR WORTHY OF THE EVENTFUL DAY, AND ANIMATING BY HIS EXAMPLE THE VICTORIOUS EFFORTS OF HIS GALLANT CREW.

AT THE CAPTURE OF THE CITY OF ST. DOMINGO

HE ACQUIRED ADDITIONAL DISTINCTION BY THE GREAT ABILITY WITH WHICH HE CONDUCTED THE OPERATIONS OF THE NAVAL FORCE, AND BY HIS HUMANITY TO THE VANQUISHED IN THEIR SURRENDER TO THE BRITISH ARMS.

IN HIS PROFESSION HIS CONSIDERATE CARE FOR THE COMFORTS OF THOSE UNDER HIS COMMAND SECURED TO HIM THE SERVICE OF ATTACHED HEARTS.

IN PRIVATE LIFE HIS CHEERFUL TEMPER AND SOCIAL KINDNESS ENDEARED HIM TO ALL CLASSES IN AND AROUND THIS VILLAGE, WHERE HIS VIRTUES AND UNAFFECTED PIETY DIFFUSED THE CALM ENJOYMENTS OF DOMESTIC PEACE OVER HIS HAPPY HOME.

Monarca (74), she engaged the French *L'Aigle*. Their masts became entangled and a fast and furious fight ensued.

The crew of *L'Aigle*, supplemented by 150 soldiers, was well trained in the use of musketry and grenades. At such close range, the *Bellerophon*'s upper decks became a killing zone, so much so that Cumby suggested that his captain, John Cooke, should remove his epaulettes for fear that they marked him out. Cooke declined. A short while later, he instructed Cumby to order the gun captains to keep the starboard guns firing at all costs. On his return Cumby, choking from the thick, acrid smoke that stifled the gun decks, met two sailors carrying the master, Mr Overton, whom Cumby had last seen standing next to Captain Cooke on the quarterdeck. Overton had been mortally wounded and his leg was horribly shattered. Cumby next encountered the quartermaster, who had come to inform him that Cooke was very badly wounded, hit twice in the chest by musket balls while reloading his pistols. When at last Cumby reached the quarterdeck, Cooke was dead. His last words were conveyed to him: 'Let me lie quietly one minute. Tell Lieutenant Cumby never to strike!'

All of a sudden, his senses reeling from the din and amidst the fiercest of fights, Cumby found himself in command of the veteran *Bellerophon*. It was a quarter past one o'clock. Only in retrospect would he learn that her situation was at that very moment graver than any other British ship during the whole of the battle. He ordered all the remaining men down from the poop deck, and, calling boarders, had them muster in readiness to repel any attempts the enemy might make to board, 'their position rendering it quite impracticable for us to board them in the face of such musketry.' The French grenades were dangerously effective. At one point, Cumby picked up one from the gangway while the fuse was burning and threw it overboard.

Whatever advantages the French had on the upper decks, Cumby realised they were more than compensated for by the superiority of the *Bellerophon*'s fire on the lower and main decks. This was vigorously maintained and *L'Aigle*'s great guns eventually ceased firing. The crisis passed, the *Bellerophon* came through with twenty-seven killed and 127 wounded, but Cumby had fulfilled his captain's last command.

After Trafalgar, Cumby was promoted captain. His next recorded action was on 14 November 1808, in command of the *Polyphemus* (64), when his men cut out the French schooner *Colibri* (3) from San Domingo Harbour, in the West Indies. Then, in July of the following year, he was given charge of a squadron consisting of the *Polyphemus*, *Aurora* (46) and eight small craft ordered to blockade San Domingo. The *Polyphemus* landed eight of her lower-deck guns for service in the shore batteries. The blockade was so successful that the French governor opened negotiations for capitulation.

A quiet period followed. Cumby was made a Companion of the Bath in 1831 and his last posting was to superintendent of Pembroke Dockyard, where he died on 27 September 1837.

PW

HENRY DIGBY

(1770–1842)
Captain HMS *Africa*

Henry Digby was the eldest son of the Honourable and Very Reverend William Digby, Dean of Durham and Chaplain Ordinary to George III.

He was born in Bath on 20 January 1770, and entered the service in 1783 as a midshipman under Admiral Innes on board the *Europa* (50) bound for the West Indies. He was promoted lieutenant in 1790. In 1795, whilst a lieutenant in the *Pallas*, he performed valuable service in saving lives when HMS *Boyne* was lost by fire. He was promoted commander in 1795, and in command of the *Incendiary* sloop, and later the small frigate *Aurora*, he made several valuable captures in 1796.

He was made post on 19 December 1796, and in 1798 commanded the *Leviathan*, a Third Rate bearing the broad pennant of Commodore Duckworth, and served at the capture of Minorca, defended by a Spanish garrison of some 3,500 men. They took the island without loss of life, finding at Port Mahon a wealth of naval stores, a brig on the stocks, fourteen gunboats and several merchant vessels.

In 1799, Digby was appointed to the frigate *Alcmène*, in which he cruised between the coast of Portugal and the Azores, making numerous important captures. Most importantly, on 18 October 1799, in company with the frigates *Naiad* and *Triton*, he assisted in the capture of the rich Spanish treasure ship *Santa Brigada* (36), out of Vera Cruz and bound for Spain carrying a cargo of $1,400,000. Digby's share of the prize money for all these captures made him a rich man. He remained on the Lisbon and Mediterranean stations until 1801, when he was given command of the large frigate *Resistance* and moved to North America. On the outward passage in 1801, he captured the French privateer *Elizabeth* en route from Cayenne to Bordeaux. It proved to be last vessel taken before the Peace of Amiens. He returned to England on 30 November the same year, and was employed that winter in the Channel searching for smugglers.

At Trafalgar, Digby commanded HMS *Africa* (64). Although one of the smallest battleships present at the action, she played one of the most remarkable and courageous roles in the battle. During the early morning of the 21st, Digby appears to have lost sight of the fleet. When firing commenced, he found himself separated from the rest of the British fleet, and likewise alarmingly close to the *Neptuno*, the leading ship of the enemy van. Nelson signalled the *Africa* to make all possible sail, but Digby seems to have interpreted the order – which was intended to take him out of danger – as meaning that he was to engage the enemy more closely. Accordingly, he made his way along the Franco-Spanish line, exchanging broadsides with various ships, until he came up before the massive *Santissima Trinidad* (130), then already engaged with a number of other British ships. Thinking that she had surrendered, he sent on board his first

Date of death: 19 August 1842

Place of death: Minterne House, Minterne Magna, Dorset

Where buried: St Andrew's Church, Minterne Magna, Dorset

Description: A family grave to the left of the west door of the Church. A square plot, surrounded by low railings. The grave itself has sloping sides with a flat top surmounted by a flat carved stone cross. There is a carved inscription to one of the vertical sides below the railing. The grave is maintained by the present Lord and Lady Digby.

Dimensions: Approx 300 cm square

Transcription

BENEATH THIS STONE LIE

ADMIRAL HON ROBERT DIGBY DIED FEBRUARY 27 1814

ELINOR WIFE OF THE ABOVE DIED JULY 28 1830 AGED 74

ADMIRAL SIR HENRY DIGBY DIED AUGUST 19 1842 AGED 72

JANE ELIZABETH DOWAGER VISCOUNTESS ANDOVER WIFE OF THE ABOVE

DIED APRIL 29 1863 AGED 86

[OTHER NAMES UNCLEAR]

lieutenant, John Smith, to take possession of her. Smith reached her quarterdeck before realising that she had not surrendered at all. Even so, in those comparatively chivalrous days, the boarding party was permitted to withdraw unmolested.

When the ships of Dumanoir's squadron finally completed their turn and approached the centre of the battle, the *Africa* engaged with the French *Intrépide* (74), and for about forty minutes fought her steadily, until HMS *Orion* arrived on her starboard quarter and assisted in silencing her. The *Africa*'s masts and yards had been substantially mauled and her rigging and sails cut to pieces; while her hull was seriously damaged, including several holes on the waterline. She had suffered sixty-two casualties, including seven officers.

Digby received the naval gold medal and a sword from the Lloyd's Patriotic Fund. He was created a CB in 1815, was promoted rear admiral in 1819, vice admiral in 1830 and admiral in 1841. He was advanced to KCB in 1831 and GCB in 1842, and was commander-in-chief at Sheerness in 1840–1. He died at Minterne, Dorset, in 1842 and was buried there.

AJC

BRASS PLAQUE
Location: St Andrew's Church,
  Minterne Magna, Dorset
  On the wall of the south aisle.
Description: Brass tablet. Some initial
  letters are in red.
Dimensions: 100 cm x 150 cm

Transcription

In memory of Sir Henry Digby GCB
Admiral of the Blue, born Jany 20 1770
died August 19 1842
  He commanded H.M.S. Africa in
the memorable action off Cape Trafalgar
October 21 1805, by his gallantry and
daring obtained the marked approbation
of the Admiral Horatio, Viscount Nelson
and the thanks of Parliament.
Also of his wife Jane Elizabeth,
eldest daughter of Thomas William Coke,
Earl of Leicester and relict of Charles
Nevinson,
Viscount Andover, born December 22 1777,
died April 29 1863.

In testimony of their sincere and dutiful
affection their sons Edward St Vincent,
Lord Digby, and the Hon and Rev Kenelm
Henry Digby MA have caused this memorial
to be erected.

George Duff
(1764–1805)
Captain HMS *Mars*

George Duff and Nelson did not meet until shortly before Trafalgar. Nonetheless, Duff's reputation was such that Nelson showed him considerable respect, placing him in positions of responsibility ahead of more senior officers.

Duff was born in 1764 in the small coastal town of Banff in north-east Scotland, and from an early age showed a passion for the sea, once managing to stow away in a merchant ship; fortunately its voyage was short. He entered the Navy at thirteen, sailing with his great uncle, Rear Admiral (later Vice Admiral) Robert Duff, commander-in-chief of the Mediterranean station, in HMS *Panther*. In the next six years, he saw action thirteen times, including (in HMS *Montagu*) the Battle of the Saintes (12 April 1782). Commissioned lieutenant on 15 September 1779, he was promoted commander on 21 September 1790 with the support of his relative, the Earl of Fife, and the jurist and statesman Henry Dundas (later Viscount Melville and First Lord of the Admiralty). His post captaincy followed on 9 February 1793.

By then he was married and a father. He and his 'childhood sweetheart', Sophie Dirom, wed in 1791, settling in Castle Street, Edinburgh; their only child, a boy named Norwich, was born in 1792. As captain, Duff successively commanded HM ships *Duke*, *Vengeance*, *Glenmore* and – lastly and fatefully – *Mars* (74), which he joined in May 1804.

Duff had few complaints about the *Mars*: he thought her 'in every respect a very good ship,' weatherly (able to steer closer to the wind than the average), easy in a sea, responsive to the helm, and a much better sailer 'than the generality of ships.' If only he could bring her onto a more even keel, he said, he was sure she would be even better.

Somewhat unusually, he laid down rules of uniform for his men, insisting they be mustered once a week and inspected for cleanliness; and on taking command of the *Mars*, he set about another kind of uniformity favoured by Scots in the contemporary Royal Navy, introducing as many of his countrymen as possible into the gunroom and wardroom. Having inherited an existing set of officers, this was not as easy as in the *Glenmore*, where he had had only one rather lonely English lieutenant, but he still managed to bring in seven Scots, including two of his cousins and his son: Norwich joined the ship off Cadiz in 1805, shortly before his thirteenth birthday.

Whenever away from home Duff wrote daily to his wife, but sadly for posterity the letters were routinely destroyed on his return; their quantity seemed too great to keep, and only those from his last voyage survive. Off Cadiz, he was immediately charmed by Nelson, writing on 1 October, 'I dined with his Lordship yesterday and had a very merry dinner. He certainly is the pleasantest Admiral I ever served under,' and later added the telling observation that 'we all wish to do what he likes, without any kind of orders.' On 4 October, placed in charge of the Inshore Squadron, he became a key part of the chain of communications between the frigates stationed close to Cadiz and the fleet, positioned about fifty miles westward. He recognised the privilege: 'I have been myself very lucky with most of my Admirals, but…even this little detachment is a kind thing to me, there being so many senior officers to me in the Fleet, as it shows his attention, and wish to bring me forward.'

At 6am on 20 October, Duff sent the signal, 'I have discovered a strange fleet' – a standard message, but one whose special meaning under the circumstances was instantly understood – and at 8.32am the frigate *Phoebe* signalled, 'The enemy's ships have put to sea', meaning that the majority of the Combined Fleet was now out of harbour. At 1.50pm, 'when there could be no question of their turning back,' Duff repeated the message to the fleet.

With that, Nelson's inspired but carefully worked out plan swung into action, and on the morning of 21 October it took visible shape. In Collingwood's words, it was 'an impetuous attack in two distinct bodies… The weather line he commanded and left the Lee Line totally to my direction.' This was not entirely true: at 9.41am Nelson signalled the *Mars*, close behind Collingwood's *Royal Sovereign*, to take station astern of the flagship. At 10am, he went further and ordered Duff to 'Head the larboard column', repeating the order at 10.45am. But the *Mars* could not overtake the *Royal Sovereign* and in fact was third into the battle. 'The light wind was unfavourable to us,' wrote Collingwood. 'I thought it a long time after I got through their line before I found my friends about me: Duff, worthy Duff, was next to me but found a difficulty in getting through for we had to make a kind of S to pass them in the manner they were formed… .'

Meanwhile, in the long slow approach to battle, Duff had grasped the opportunity to write quickly to his 'dearest Sophia':

I have just time to tell you we are going into Action with the Combined Fleet.
I hope and trust in God that we shall all behave as become us, and that I may

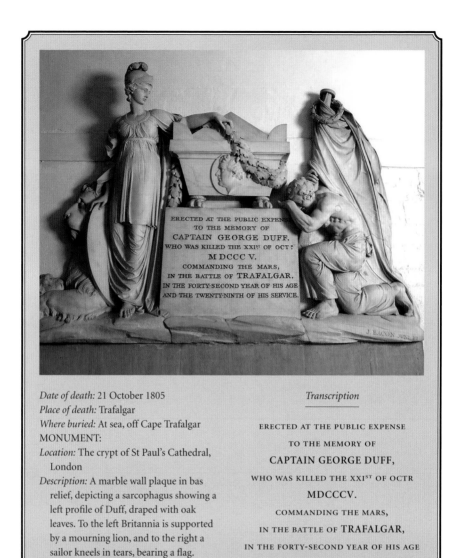

ERECTED AT THE PUBLIC EXPENSE
TO THE MEMORY OF
CAPTAIN GEORGE DUFF,
WHO WAS KILLED THE XXIST OF OCTR
M DCCC V.
COMMANDING THE MARS,
IN THE BATTLE OF TRAFALGAR,
IN THE FORTY-SECOND YEAR OF HIS AGE
AND THE TWENTY-NINTH OF HIS SERVICE.

J. BACON JUN

Date of death: 21 October 1805
Place of death: Trafalgar
Where buried: At sea, off Cape Trafalgar
MONUMENT:
Location: The crypt of St Paul's Cathedral, London
Description: A marble wall plaque in bas relief, depicting a sarcophagus showing a left profile of Duff, draped with oak leaves. To the left Britannia is supported by a mourning lion, and to the right a sailor kneels in tears, bearing a flag.
Sculptor: J Bacon Jnr.
Dimensions: 350 cm x 261 cm.

Transcription

ERECTED AT THE PUBLIC EXPENSE
TO THE MEMORY OF
CAPTAIN GEORGE DUFF,
WHO WAS KILLED THE XXIST OF OCTR
MDCCCV.
COMMANDING THE MARS,
IN THE BATTLE OF **TRAFALGAR,**
IN THE FORTY-SECOND YEAR OF HIS AGE
AND THE TWENTY-NINTH OF HIS SERVICE.

yet have the happiness of taking my beloved wife and children in my arms. Norwich is quite well and happy. I have, however, ordered him off the quarter-deck. Yours ever, and most truly…

But it was his last letter; he was one the battle's fairly early victims. Having endured long-distance fire from four enemy warships, the *Mars* was directly engaged with two, the *Fougeaux* and the *Pluton*, when a broadside came from one or the other and, wrote Midshipman James Robinson (himself, like Duff, a native of Banff), 'It was then the gallant Captain fell. I saw him fall. His head and neck were taken entirely off his body… .'

In a bizarre gesture of defiance, the crew held up his body 'and gave three cheers to show they were not discouraged,' then returned to their guns under the command of Duff's first lieutenant, William Hennah. The corpse lay on deck for the rest of the battle, covered with a Union flag, and afterwards thirteen-year-old Norwich Duff wrote a most touching message on paper that had first been carefully lined in pencil:

> *My Dear Mama, You cannot possibly imagine how unwilling I am to begin this melancholy letter. However as you must unavoidably hear of the fate of dear Papa, I write these few lines to request you to bear it as patiently as you can. He died like a hero, having gallantly led his ship into action…*

Apart from Nelson, Duff was one of only two officers to be named by Collingwood in his Trafalgar Dispatch, the other being Captain John Cooke of the *Bellerophon*, who was also killed in the battle. Duff was buried at sea and a memorial was raised in St Paul's Cathedral. Sophie Duff had to console herself with her husband's naval gold medal and a handsome silver vase from the Lloyd's Patriotic Fund. Norwich Duff remained a professional naval officer all his life and died in the rank of vice admiral on 20 April 1862.

SWRH

Tomb of Vice Admiral Thomas Dundas. (See over for transcription).

THOMAS DUNDAS

Date of death: 29 March 1841
Place of death: Reading
Where buried: St Nicholas Church, Hurst,
   near Reading
Description: A stone box tomb at the western
   edge of the graveyard, surrounded by iron
   railings. A family grave, shared with his
   wife and other family members.
   Inscriptions are carved on the top and on
   two sides though these are largely illegible.
Dimensions: Tomb: 109 cm high, 100 cm
   wide x 184 cm long.
   Railings: 122 cm high, 205 cm wide x 290
   cm long.

Transcription

[part only]
VICE ADMIRAL
THOMAS DUNDAS

[EAST END PANEL]
LADY DUNDAS
DIED AT READING
SEPT 10TH 1848
IN THE [NUMBER] YEAR OF HER AGE

THOMAS DUNDAS
(1758–1841)
Captain HMS *Naiad*

Thomas Dundas joined the Royal Navy on 23 May 1778, when he was entered as captain's servant on HMS *Suffolk*. A year later, he joined HMS *Alfred* and was soon made midshipman. Over the next few years, he served in HMS *Fame*, *Formidable* and *Edgar* before passing for lieutenant in November 1788. However, he did not obtain his lieutenant's commission until war with France broke out in 1793. Two years later, he was promoted commander and then captain in 1798. In 1799, when commanding the West Indiaman *La Prompte*, he captured the Spanish ship *Urca Cargadora*. He was appointed captain of HMS *Naiad* in 1804 and remained in command of her until 1808. In 1825, he was promoted rear admiral and then vice admiral in 1837. He was created KCB in 1831 and died on 29 March 1841.

In August 1805, during the campaign before Trafalgar, the *Naiad* spotted the Combined Fleet, was chased by them but escaped to bring the news to Admiral Cornwallis. Shortly before Trafalgar, Nelson put Dundas and the *Naiad* under Blackwood's (HMS *Euryalus*) command as part of the frigate squadron that became the 'eyes of the fleet'. The *Naiad* was one of the frigates watching Cadiz for any sign of the Combined Fleet making a move. On 19 October, the Combined Fleet set sail and the *Naiad* repeated the signals from the *Euryalus* to that effect. For the next two days the frigates shadowed the Combined Fleet, reporting their moves back to Nelson. On the day of Trafalgar, the *Naiad* took station to the windward of the weather column but took no direct part in the action except to repeat signals. She helped in rescuing men from disabled ships and took the dismasted HMS *Belleisle* in tow when that ship became unmanageable.

NS

Philip Charles Durham

(1763–1845)
Captain HMS *Defiance*

Philip Durham was born in Largo, Fifeshire, in 1763. His naval career began on board the *Trident* in 1777 and in the following year he sailed for America under command of the tyrannical Captain Molloy. With a ship near mutiny, the following year was a trial for young Durham. Fortunately, he managed to be returned to England and gained a billet on board the *Edgar*, Captain Elliot, and took part in the relief of Gibraltar in 1781. Durham next served on board the *Victory* and was selected by Admiral Kempenfelt to assist with signals, staying with Kempenfelt when he moved to the *Royal George*. When the great ship sank at Spithead on 29 April 1782, the admiral lost his life but Durham was saved.

Durham soon joined the *Union*, still as acting lieutenant, and in her, as part of Lord Howe's fleet, again relieved Gibraltar. This was followed by a cruise to the West Indies and he was confirmed in the rank of lieutenant and appointed to the *Raisonable*, cruising off the west coast of Africa. But with the end of the war and failing health, Durham went on leave, and for two years lived in France, learning the language and enjoying French society.

Returning to sea under the command of Commodore Elliot, Durham served in several ships until November 1790, when he was given command of the *Daphne*. In February 1793, with the commencement of war with France, he had command of the *Spitfire* and made his first capture: the French privateer *Afrique*. The next year was most active: moving to a couple of ships until in the *Hind*, he managed to bring a convoy of 157 ships home safely from the Mediterranean. With this success, Captain Durham was now appointed to HMS *Anson* (46), one of the largest frigates in the Royal Navy, and stayed with her during the next six years, taking part in John Borlase Warren's action of 12 October 1798, for which he received the naval small gold medal.

In April 1803, Durham was appointed to the *Defiance* (74) and in her served with Cornwallis's Channel Fleet off Brest. On 22 July 1805, the *Defiance* played an important role as part of Sir Robert Calder's squadron which intercepted the combined squadrons of France and Spain off Cape Finisterre upon their return from the West Indies. As the *Defiance* was probably the fastest 74 in Calder's squadron, she had been sent to the west to search for the approaching enemy. The *Defiance* found them and was able to alert Calder through the firing of guns. Calder changed course to intercept the enemy, and the *Defiance* took her station in the line. A spirited action of four hours ensued with the *Defiance* taking several shot between wind and water and her rigging being much cut up. The weather had turned to fog, which also made the action difficult for the ships of Calder's squadron to see each other. In these conditions, when the opposing fleets separated, Calder decided to regroup and secure the two prizes he had captured.

The following morning, the *Defiance* was stationed between the two fleets. Durham signalled repeatedly to Calder, trying to indicate that a renewed attack was possible; but he was ignored and later, when he reported on board the flagship, was reprimanded for being 'over zealous'. The *Defiance* was so badly damaged that she was ordered home for repairs and, while in London, Durham met Nelson in the Admiralty waiting room. Nelson apparently told him, 'I am sorry your ship is not ready, I should have been very glad to have you.' Durham replied, 'Ask Lord Barham to place me under your Lordship's orders, and I will soon be ready.' Nelson duly did so, and Durham joined him off Cadiz on 7 October.

Even then he might have missed the battle. Having learned that he was being criticised for his conduct in the battle off Finisterre, Calder had asked for a court martial and went home, taking with him as witnesses some of the captains who had served with him at the battle. However, when Durham discovered that he was not under direct orders to accompany his admiral, he declined to go and stayed with his ship.

So it was that Durham, in the *Defiance*, found himself on the morning of 21 October, toward the rear of Collingwood's column, just astern of the *Revenge*. Entering the fray, Durham quickly moved to engage Gravina's flagship, the *Principe de Asturias*, but found his way blocked by the French *Berwick* (74); the ships collided and the *Defiance* took away her bowsprit. Gravina's ship was now sailing away to leeward with the *Berwick* trying to follow her.

The *Defiance* was now much cut up, particularly in the rigging, when she came upon the French *L'Aigle* (80), which had previously been raked by the *Bellerophon*, *Belleisle* and *Revenge*. After a fierce gunnery duel, Durham noticed the French fire had begun to slacken, so he called for boarders, only to find that all his boats had been shot through. Inspired by a gallant young Irish midshipman, Jack Spratt, who swam alone to *L'Aigle* and began the fighting, the crew of the *Defiance* swarmed aboard the French ship and eventually, after some particularly vicious hand-to-hand fighting, eventually captured her after a most gallant resistance.

Durham received wounds to his leg and side. After the battle, he received a visit from Hardy, who told him, 'I have a word of comfort for you; one of the last things Lord Nelson said before he action began, was, "Hardy, tell your friend Durham he was the most sensible man of the party to stick to his ship."

Later, he went on board the frigate *Euryalus* to see Admiral Collingwood. Observing a French officer leaning on the capstan, he discovered he was Villeneuve, who asked him if he had been in Calder's action. When Durham replied that he had, Villeneuve sighed and said, 'I wish Sir Robert and I had fought it out that day. He would not be in his present situation, nor I in mine.'

The *Defiance*, in great need of repair, was ordered to Portsmouth and, much to Durham's surprise, he was in time to testify after all at Calder's court martial. He remained in England and bore the Nelson's standard as a Knight of the Bath

Date of death: 2 April 1845

Place of death: Naples

Where buried: Largo and Newburn Parish Church, Upper Largo, Fife.
(Sir Philip's body was transported first to Malta, and then via HMS *Hecate* (Cdr Bower) to Spithead. At Portsmouth Lord Haddington gave orders for HM Steam vessel *Comet* (Lieut Prettyman) to convey the remains to Scotland).

Description: Buried beneath the west aisle of the Church. There is also a wall monument in white marble, with an inscription between two pillars, and surmounted by a semi-circular arch containing a coat of arms.

Dimensions: 285 cm x 133 cm (Wall monument)

Transcription

IN MEMORY OF

SIR PHILIP CHARLES HENDERSON CALDERWOOD DURHAM
OF FORDEL, POLTON AND LARGO.

ADMIRAL OF THE RED, KNIGHT GRAND CROSS OF THE BATH,
AND OF MILITARY MERIT IN FRANCE.

HE WAS BORN AT LARGO ON THE 29TH OF JULY 1763,
ENTERED THE ROYAL NAVY AT FOURTEEN, AND WAS MADE
POST CAPTAIN IN 1793. HIS ACTIVITY, GALLANTRY, JUDG
MENT AND ZEAL WERE EXCELLED BY NONE IN HIS PROFES
SION, AND HIS NUMEROUS CAPTURES AND SUCCESSES WERE
ACKNOWLEDGED BY MANY PUBLIC TESTIMONIALS. HE BE-
CAME REAR ADMIRAL IN 1810, WAS COMMANDER-IN-CHIEF
IN THE WEST INDIES FROM 1813 TILL THE PEACE OF 1815,
AND HELD THE COMMAND AT PORTSMOUTH FROM 1837 TO
1839, HE REPRESENTED QUEENBOROUGH AND DEVIZES
IN SEVERAL PARLIAMENTS, BUT PASSED HIS LATTER YEARS
CHIEFLY AT FORDEL, COURTED IN SOCIETY AND GENEROUS-
LY SPENDING AN AMPLE FORTUNE. IN 1799 HE MARRIED
LADY CHARLOTTE MATILDA BRUCE, DAUGHTER OF CHARLES
FIFTH EARL OF ELGIN, WHO DIED IN 1816; AND SECONDLY
IN 1817, ANNE ELIZABETH, DAUGHTER AND HEIRESS OF
SIR JOHN HENDERSON OF FORDEL BARONET, WHOM HE SUR-
VIVED ONLY THREE MONTHS. HE DIED AT NAPLES ON THE
2ND OF APRIL 1845, AND WAS INTERRED BENEATH THE
WEST AISLE OF THIS CHURCH.

ERECTED BY HIS GRAND-NEPHEW,
JAMES WOLFE MURRAY OF CRINGLETIE.

1849.

at the state funeral. He received the naval gold medal and a sword from the Lloyd's Patriotic Fund.

Later in 1806, Durham took command of the *Renown* in the Channel Fleet, and was sent to join Collingwood in the Mediterranean, where he subsequently was given a commodore's broad pendant and stayed until 1810. Upon his return home in 1810, he was made rear admiral and then in 1813, with his flag on board the *Venerable*, he became commander-in-chief of the Leeward Islands. On his way out, he managed to capture two large French frigates. In 1815, he accepted the surrender of both Martinique and Guadeloupe.

Following the conclusion of the war, the usual honours followed, including the GCB and the rank of full admiral. Durham married twice but bore no heirs. In 1845, he was on tour in Italy, where acute bronchitis brought an end to his life in Naples on 2 April 1845. His body was brought home and buried at Largo.

SCC

THOMAS FRANCIS FREMANTLE
(1765–1819)
Captain HMS *Neptune*

Thomas Fremantle first served under Nelson at the siege of Bastia in 1794, when in command of HMS *Tartar* (28), and became a close friend and colleague. Their friendship continued until the day of Nelson's death at Trafalgar, when Fremantle was close astern of the *Victory* in the battleship HMS *Neptune*. When Nelson died, he lost a friend who, as he told his wife, 'appreciated my Abilities and Zeal'.

His ability was noted early by Nelson, and was confirmed with the taking of the *Ca Ira* (80) in Hotham's action in March 1795. The Frenchman had lost some rigging in a collision, so Fremantle brought his little frigate HMS *Inconstant* (36) under her stern and put in two broadsides, but sustained damage himself until Nelson in HMS *Agamemnon* (64) arrived to his rescue.

In the following months, Nelson and Fremantle saw plenty of action together along the Italian coast. They supported the Austrian army, captured

French ships at Langueglia and Alassio in 1795, and evacuated British merchants to Corsica, and took Elba in 1796. Fremantle was in Nelson's barge in the fight against the Spanish gunboats at Cadiz in June 1797, and they landed together at Santa Cruz de Tenerife in July 1797, where they were both badly wounded in the arm. They took passage home in Fremantle's ship HMS *Seahorse* (38), nursed by Fremantle's new wife, Betsey, to whom Nelson wrote his first note with his left hand. Although Fremantle's arm was saved, he never recovered the full use of it.

Fremantle had met Betsey in 1796, when he rescued her family, the Wynnes, from the advancing French armies at Leghorn in 1796. Betsey was eighteen, Catholic, and an heiress; Tom was thirty-one, Protestant, and poor. She had to ward off the attentions of another of Nelson's friends, Thomas Foley, 'that grey headed gallant', but her love for Fremantle triumphed, and they were eventually married in Lady Hamilton's drawing room in Naples. Prince Augustus, youngest son of George III, gave away the bride.

Betsey described her husband as 'good natured, kind, amiable, lively, with qualities to win everyone's heart the first moment one sees him'. He was also 'short, stocky, not handsome, but with fiery black eyes which are quite captivating'. His letters home to Betsey are a delight to read, but to his men he was a strict disciplinarian, who imposed high standards. He introduced petty courts of enquiry for defaulters; a measure adopted sixty years later by the Royal Navy.

Fremantle served in Nelson's attacking squadron at Copenhagen in 1801, commanding HMS *Ganges* (74), where he distinguished himself in a hard-fought battle. He was back in the *Ganges* in 1803 fulfilling the Navy's main function of preventing Napoleon's planned invasion, stationed off south-west Ireland and enduring gales and desertions. He then moved to blockade Ferrol until the end of 1804, when his ship was paid off. He took command of HMS *Neptune* (98) in May 1805, and was then diverted south to assist in the blockade of the Combined Fleet in Cadiz.

The next two months of patrolling off Cadiz seemed interminable and, writing to Betsey, Fremantle thought they would be 'here 'til doomsday!' He was invigorated by the arrival of Nelson, and the 'flattering' allocation of his 'Old Station as his Second'. This meant frequent visits to HMS *Victory*.

At Trafalgar, the *Neptune* was the third ship in Nelson's line. Fremantle first engaged the *Bucentaure* as he passed under her stern and then, having carefully placed his ship on the quarter of the massive *Santissima Trinidad* (130), held his position and engaged her in a long gunnery duel: a feat reported by Midshipman Robinson as 'the most seamanlike act I witnessed that day'. Although other ships assisted him, he always claimed that she surrendered to him. During the storm, desperate attempts were made to save the massive Spanish ship, but eventually she had to be scuttled after all her crew had been saved. Before she sank, Fremantle took the fittings from her chapel to adorn his home church at Swanbourne. He towed HMS *Victory* to Gibraltar, and employed

Date of death: 19th December 1819
Place of death: Naples
Where buried: Naples, on 23rd December, with
full military honours. Grave only recently
discovered. See Addendum, page 127.
MONUMENT:
Location: SE corner of the Upper Barracca
Garden, Valletta, Malta
Description: Above the plinth is a rectangular
block about 1.83 cm high, and 76 cm wide
bearing an inscription, on three sides. Above is
a stone urn similar to a Patriotic Fund vase
without handles.
Note: Erected in Malta because the political
situation in Naples at the time was too
unstable for it to be erected there.

Transcription

SACRED TO THE MEMORY
OF SIR THOMAS FRANCIS FREMANTLE
KNIGHT GRAND CROSS
OF THE
BATH, GUELPH, SAINT FERDINAND AND MERIT,
SAINT MICHAEL AND SAINT GEORGE,
KNIGHT COMMANDER OF MARIA THERESA,
BARON OF THE AUSTRIAN EMPIRE,
AND VICE ADMIRAL OF THE BLUE,
WHO DIED AT NAPLES IN THE CHIEF COMMAND
OF HIS MAJESTY'S NAVAL FORCES
IN THE MEDITERRANEAN
ON THE 19 DECR 1819 IN THE 54 YEAR OF HIS AGE.
THIS MONUMENT IS ERECTED BY CAPTAIN A P GREEN
AND THE OFFICERS OF HIS MAJESTY'S SHIP ROCHFORT
IN WHICH HE HAD HIS FLAG
AS A TESTIMONY OF THEIR RESPECT
FOR HIS CHARACTER AND TALENTS

RESTORED BY
HIS GRAND NEPHEW
H.E. GEN SIR ARTHUR FREMANTLE K.C.M.G.C.B.
GOVERNOR OF MALTA
1895

RESTORED BY
HIS GREAT-GRANDCHILDREN
1938

Villeneuve's flag captain, Magendie, to draw a plan of the battle for posterity. A year later, he returned home to become a Lord of the Admiralty, and MP for Sandwich.

Promoted rear admiral in 1810, he took command in the Adriatic until the end of the Napoleonic Wars. Fiume, Trieste and every place on the coasts of Dalmatia, Croatia, Istria and Friuli surrendered to his squadron, and almost 800 vessels and a thousand guns were taken or destroyed. For these services, he was made a KCB and a Baron of the Austrian States in 1815, rising to GCB in 1818. In 1819, he was promoted vice admiral and appointed Commander-in-Chief Mediterranean. But he did not enjoy his fortune long, for he died suddenly in December 1819. He was buried in Naples with full military honours by order of the King of Naples. His obituary stated that 'few men possessed a more kind and generous heart.'

CAF

RICHARD GRINDALL
(1750–1820)
Captain HMS *Prince*

Grindall is one of the Trafalgar Captains of whom little is known. He had a worthy but unremarkable career before the battle and fell quickly into obscurity after it. Moreover, his ship, HMS *Prince*, played little part in the action: in the words of Lieutenant Frederick Hoffman of HMS *Tonnant*, she 'sailed like a Haystack.'

Born in 1750, Grindall entered the Royal Navy in the late 1760s/early 1770s, becoming a lieutenant in 1776. As a young man, he served mainly in battleships, including Sir Samuel Hood's flagship, HMS *Barfleur*, in the West Indies in 1781. Promoted post captain in 1783, he started the war against France in command of HMS *Thalia* and then moved to the battleship HMS *Irresistible* in 1795 and took part in Lord Bridport's action off Groix.

Taking command of the *Prince* in 1803, he served in her with the Channel Fleet off Brest until he was detached, with Calder in August 1805, to blockade Cadiz. At Trafalgar, the *Prince* sailed so slowly that she was ordered to act independently and finally managed to get into action around 4pm. Having exchanged broadsides briefly with Gravina's flagship, the *Principe de Asturias*, she assisted in the destruction of the French battleship *Achille* which, having caught fire, blew up at the end of the battle. Grindall lowered his boats and managed to save some of her crew. Later, during the storm, he and his crew managed to save 350 men from the stricken *Santissima Trinidad*.

Grindall received the naval gold medal and a sword from the Lloyd's Patriotic Fund and, as one of the most senior captains present at the battle, became a rear admiral in the general promotion of 9 November. He never served at sea again, becoming a vice admiral and a KCB before he died on 23 May 1820.

CSW

Date of death: 23 May 1820
Place of death: Wickham, Hants
Where buried: St Nicholas Church, Wickham, Hants
41 yds north of west door of church.
Description: Family grave consisting of a flat gravestone with 2 upright headstones and 2 footstones, all mounted on a large stone plinth which has the vestiges of iron railings (probably removed in WW2). The LH upright contains an inscription to Midshipman Edmund Grindall, youngest son of Sir Richard, and the RH upright contains one to Lt Festing Horatio Grindall, 3rd son of Sir Richard. The flat stone is dedicated to Sir Richard and his wife Katherine. Unfortunately all these inscriptions are now virtually illegible.
Dimensions: Base plinth: 201 cm x 289 cm
Gravestone: 101 cm x 184 cm
Each headstone: 75 cm x 160 cm
Each footstone: 47 cm x 44 cm

Transcription

[NB As the inscriptions are illegible, the following transcriptions have been obtained from the Church Registers, and do not follow the layout on the stones]

LH Upright:

HERE LIES DEPOSITED THE REMAINS OF MR EDMUND GRINDALL, MIDSHIPMAN RN, YOUNGEST SON OF VICE ADMIRAL GRINDALL AND KATHERINE HIS WIFE, WHO DEPARTED THIS LIFE 21 SEPTEMBER 1811 AGE 20

RH Upright:

HERE LIES DEPOSITED THE BODY OF LT FESTING HORATIO GRINDALL, RN, 3RD SON OF VICE ADMIRAL GRINDALL AND KATHERINE HIS WIFE, WHO DEPARTED THIS LIFE 23 MAY 1812 AGE 25

Gravestone:

ALSO THE REMAINS OF SIR RICHARD GRINDALL, ADMIRAL, RN, WHO DIED 23 MAY 1820 AGE 69, ALSO KATHERINE HIS WIFE WHO DIED 6 FEBRUARY 1831 AGE 72

THOMAS MASTERMAN HARDY

(1769–1839)
Captain HMS *Victory*

Hardy will always be best remembered for the part he played in the company of Nelson at the Battle of Trafalgar on board HMS *Victory* but his career encompassed very much more. He spent fifty-eight years of his life serving his country in the Royal Navy and, in the words of the inscription on his memorial at Greenwich, he was 'one of the noblest ornaments of the profession.' His features were broad and massive and he was taller than most of his contemporaries. His nature was calm, patient, slow and careful; his manner strong; his character sometimes stubborn but his mind agile; his instinct quick and decisive.

Hardy was born on 5 April 1769 at Portisham, Dorset, the sixth child and second son of Joseph Hardy and Nanny, daughter of Thomas Masterman. He entered the Navy in 1781 on board the Brig HMS *Helena* but left to attend school for three years, also spending some time in the Merchant Navy. In 1790, he decided to rejoin the Royal Navy, his first appointment being as midshipman with HMS *Hebe*.

It is probable that Hardy became known to Nelson as early as 1795, when serving as a lieutenant on HMS *Meleager*, one of Nelson's squadron off Genoa. In 1796, by then serving in HMS *La Minerve*, which at that time was flying Commodore Nelson's broad pendant, he took part in a fierce engagement with the Spanish frigate *Santa Sabina*. The ship was captured and Hardy was one of the prize crew, so when a superior Spanish squadron appeared and recaptured her, he became a prisoner of war. But his stay in Spain lasted only a few weeks, for Nelson arranged an exchange in return for the release of the captain of the *Santa Sabina*, Don Jacobo Stuart.

Hardy had only been back on board *La Minerve* for a few hours when a sailor fell overboard. Even though the ship was being chased by a Spanish squadron, Hardy went in a boat to try and save the man. Discovering that he had drowned, he and his boat's crew were struggling to regain their ship but found that they were being carried by the strong current towards the Spanish. Seeing what was happening, Nelson declared, 'By God, I'll not lose Hardy,' and surprised the Spanish by ordering the ship to be hove to. Seeing this, the Spanish hesitated long enough to allow them to pick up Hardy and his men.

A few weeks later, Hardy took part in the Battle of Cape St Vincent on board

HMS *La Minerve*, and shortly after captured the brig *La Mutine* in a gallant cutting-out operation at Tenerife, for which he was promoted commander and given command of his own prize. In 1798, he took part in the campaign and Battle of the Nile and was promoted post captain by Nelson, who then took him into the *Vanguard* as his flag captain. So began the close bond between him and Nelson as he followed the admiral into HMS *Foudroyant* for the Neapolitan campaign of 1799, and then to the Baltic in 1801 when he was captain of HMS *St George*.

They then had a short time apart until, in May 1803, Hardy commissioned the *Victory* as Nelson's flagship. He served throughout the Mediterranean campaign of 1803–5 and the great chase to the West Indies in the summer of 1805. By then Hardy was unwell and when the *Victory* returned to Britain in August, he went home on leave. However, he rejoined Nelson at Portsmouth in September and so was with him at Trafalgar. In Nelson's final hour, with the battle won, Hardy reported the state of the battle to his commander and took Nelson's hand in congratulation of his brilliant victory, telling him that possibly fourteen or fifteen prizes had been taken. 'That is well, but I had bargained for twenty,' was Nelson's reply. The final moments of his master's life were passing when Nelson said, 'Take care of my dear Lady Hamilton; take care of poor Lady Hamilton. Kiss me, Hardy.' Hardy knelt down and kissed him on the cheek. Nelson said, 'Now, I am satisfied thank God, I have done my duty.' Hardy stood for a moment in silent contemplation, then he knelt once more and kissed his friend's forehead. Nelson asked, 'Who is that?' 'It is Hardy.' 'God bless you, Hardy.' Hardy withdrew and returned to the quarterdeck, never to see his commander and friend alive again. He took the battered *Victory* home and carried the 'Banner of Emblems' at the state funeral in January 1806.

For his part in the great victory at Cape Trafalgar, Hardy was created a baronet, received the naval gold medal, a silver vase from the Patriotic Fund, and a presentation sword from the City of London.

After Trafalgar, he served at Lisbon 1809–12, the North American station 1812/13 and 1815, the South American station 1819–34, became colonel, Royal Marines 1821, rear admiral 1825, was appointed First Lord of the Admiralty 1830–4, decorated GCB 1834, became Governor of Greenwich Hospital 1834–9 and, finally, Elder Brother of Trinity House 1837.

On 20 September 1839, following his usual walk around the Greenwich Hospital grounds, he was seized with strong internal pains and in a few hours the solemn tolling of the hospital bell signalled that the name of Vice Admiral Thomas Masterman Hardy was now associated with the departed heroes of our country.

Hardy's body is buried within the Georgian Mausoleum at Greenwich, adjacent to the National Maritime Museum, at the end, still, a sailor among sailors.

AGW

Date of death: 20 September 1839
Place of death: Greenwich
Where buried: The Mausoleum, Greenwich
(now part of the University of
Greenwich)
Description: The Mausoleum is a detached
brick building in the grounds of
Devonport House, Greenwich. The
entrance to the vault is now bricked up. A
plaque (transcription right) has been
fixed to the external wall of the
Mausoleum.
Dimensions: 700 cm x 650 cm

Signature of Thomas Hardy

Transcription

SACRED
TO THE MEMORY OF
**SIR THOMAS MASTERMAN
HARDY BT., G.C.B.**

Vice-Admiral of the Blue
1769 – 1839
Flag-captain and friend of
Horatio, Viscount Nelson
Governor of Greenwich Hospital
1834 – 1839

Hic jacet sepultus

"England expects that every man
will do his duty"

[The monument owned by the National Trust at Portesham, Dorset is outside the scope of this publication].

BUST

Location: At the entrance to the Chapel of the Royal Naval College, Greenwich.

Description: Made of white marble in 1843, a bust of the head and upper torso of Hardy, without arms, with an inscription below, and the whole standing on a low plinth.

Dimensions: Bust: 229 cm x 74 cm. Plinth: 86 cm x 37 cm.

Sculptor: William Behnes (1795–1864).

Transcription

ERECTED

TO THE MEMORY OF

VICE ADMIRAL

SIR THOMAS MASTERMAN HARDY.

BARONET AND G.C.B.

GOVERNOR OF GREENWICH HOSPITAL:

THE FRIEND AND COMPANION IN ARMS OF

NELSON.

EMINENT FOR JUDGEMENT

AND SELF POSSESSION:

EVER ANXIOUS FOR THE IMPROVEMENT

OF THE SERVICE,

TO WHICH HE HAD DEVOTED HIMSELF:

EQUAL TO ALL ITS DIFFICULTIES AND DUTIES,

AND CONVERSANT WITH ITS MINUTEST DETAILS.

THE NAME OF THIS GALLANT AND

DISTINGUISHED OFFICER

WILL DESCEND TO POSTERITY,

AS ONE OF THE NOBLEST ORNAMENTS

OF THE PROFESSION,

TO WHICH ENGLAND IS SO MUCH INDEBTED

FOR SECURITY AND RENOWN.

DIED SEPTEMBER 20TH 1839,

AGED 70 YEARS.

NB. In addition, a house at 156 Durnford Street, Stonehouse, Plymouth carries a plaque with the following inscription:

HERE REPUTEDLY LIVED ADMIRAL SIR T.M.HARDY BART., G.C.B., BORN 1769

CAPTAIN OF THE FLEET AT TRAFALGAR 1805

AND WITNESS TO NELSON'S IMMORTAL DYING WORDS ABOARD H.M.S. VICTORY

'KISS ME HARDY'

FIRST SEA LORD 1830-1834

GOVERNOR GREENWICH HOSPITAL 1834

DIED 1839

WILLIAM HARGOOD

(1762–1839)
Captain HMS *Belleisle*

Like Nelson, Hargood served with HRH Prince William Henry (later King William IV) in the West Indies. The connection served him better than it did Nelson.

Born on 6 May 1762, Hargood came from a modest naval background: his father was a purser. Listed in the books of HMS *Triumph* in 1773, he actually joined the Navy in March 1775 and made a return voyage to Newfoundland before joining HMS *Bristol* under Sir Peter Parker, serving with him in North America and Jamaica, and being present at the bombardment of Fort Moultrie, Charleston (28 June 1776). Promoted lieutenant on 13 January 1780, Hargood transferred into the sloop *Port Royal* and participated in the ineffective defence of Pensacola, surrendering to the Spanish in May 1781. Service in other of HM ships followed, mostly in American and British waters, and a turning point in his career came in 1785, when he met and befriended Prince William Henry in the frigate *Hebe*.

The prince took Hargood with him as second lieutenant in the frigate HMS *Pegasus* (28) in 1786 and as first lieutenant in the frigate *Andromeda* (32) in 1788, and successfully recommended his promotion to commander, 24 June 1789. From December, Hargood commanded the sloop *Swallow* off Ireland, and was made post on 22 November 1790. Further West Indies service followed in the frigate *Hyaena* (24) until her capture on 27 May 1793 by the French frigate *Concorde* (44), distantly supported by two 74s and three more frigates.

Honourably acquitted by court martial of the loss of his ship, Hargood moved to convoy service in the North Sea, Africa and North America, then in August 1796 took command of the *Leopard* (50), from which he was ejected by her crew during the Spithead mutiny in 1797. Ten or so weeks' subsequent North Sea service in HMS *Nassau* (64) culminated in her refit after serious damage in a gale, and early in 1798, commanding HMS *Intrepid* (64), Hargood was sent in charge of a convoy to China. He remained in the East Indies until the spring of 1803.

Appointed to HMS *Belleisle* (74) in November 1803, he was unable to join his ship until the following March,

Date of death: 12 December 1839
Place of death: Royal Crescent, Bath
Where buried: Bath Abbey, under the nave, at the base of a column near the west door. The inscription has been greatly eroded by the feet of worshippers over the years.
Description: A simple gravestone.
Dimensions: Approx 45 cm x 30 cm.

Transcription:

[ILLEGIBLE] BENEATH
[ILLEGIBLE] REMAINS OF
[ILLEGIBLE] WILLIAM HARGOOD
[ILLEGIBLE] [AN]D G.C.H.

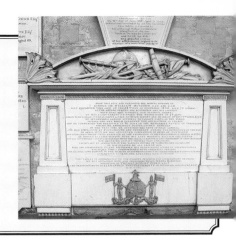

WALL PLAQUE

Location: Bath Abbey, situated on the south
wall under the 4th window from the west,
directly in front of his gravestone.

Description: A marble wall plaque, with an
inscription flanked by two pillars and
topped by a low arch containing various
naval emblems, eg anchor, globe etc.
Below the inscription is a coat of arms
with two figures bearing flags inscribed
'Belleisle' and 'Trafalgar'.

Dimensions: Approx 150 cm x 120 cm

but thenceforth came under Nelson's command until Trafalgar. He served throughout the rest of the Mediterranean campaign of 1804/5 and from April to August 1805 in the chase of Villeneuve across the Atlantic and back. Briefly attached to Cornwallis's Brest fleet, his ship was sent to Plymouth for rapid refit and returned to Nelson's Cadiz fleet on 10 October.

Although his career hitherto had been rather more marked by setbacks than successes, there can be no doubt of Hargood's bravery: insofar as it was possible in the light winds on 21 October, the *Belleisle* sped into battle and was second to enter the fray in Collingwood's lee column, fifteen to twenty minutes after the flagship *Royal Sovereign*. Under fire, with his ship visibly damaged, at least one marine decapitated by a shot and himself bruised from throat to waist, Hargood nonetheless kept the deck and with superlative nerve held his fire until the *Belleisle* was between the French *Fougueux* and the Spanish *Santa Ana*, at which he let rip a double broadside 'with the precision of a volley of musketry; upon seeing which Lord Nelson exclaimed, "Nobly done, Hargood." '

Surrounded and often fighting alone, the *Belleisle* lost thirty-three men killed and ninety-four wounded in the battle (nearly a quarter of her complement), was badly damaged in the hull and was the only British ship to be totally dismasted. One of her marines accepted the surrender of the Spanish *Argonauta* (80), bringing her second captain's sword back to Hargood. The climactic action of his life ended dramatically with the jury-rigged *Belleisle* under tow by the frigate *Naiad*, rolling awkwardly in the rising storm after the battle, as a 24-pounder cannon broke loose and crashed uncontrollably around the midnight deck.

The ship nonetheless survived, and Hargood's career was far from over. After further sea service he was made colonel of the Royal Marines, 28 April 1808; he was promoted rear admiral on 31 July 1810 and was second-in-command at Portsmouth until the following March, when he took command of the Channel Islands squadron. In 1811, he married Maria Cocks, daughter of a banker. They

NEAR THIS SPOT ARE DEPOSITED THE MORTAL REMAINS OF

ADMIRAL SIR **WILLIAM HARGOOD**, G.C.B. AND G.C.H.

WHO DEPARTED THIS LIFE ON THE 12TH DAY OF DECEMBER 1839, AGED 79 YEARS,

AFTER HAVING SERVED HIS SOVEREIGN AND HIS COUNTRY

WITH ZEAL AND FIDELITY FOR SEVENTY YEARS.

HE WAS A LIEUTENANT ON BOARD THE MAGNIFICENT OF 74 GUNS

WHICH BORE A SHARE IN THE GLORIOUS ACTION BETWEEN RODNEY AND DE GRASSE ON

THE 12TH APRIL 1782.

HE AFTERWARDS SERVED ACTIVELY IN VARIOUS PARTS OF THE WORLD

DURING THE WAR WHICH FOLLOWED THE REVOLUTION IN FRANCE

AND HE COMMANDED THE BELLEISLE OF 80 GUNS IN THE MEMORABLE

BATTLE OF TRAFALGAR

WHERE HE EMINENTLY DISTINGUISHED HIMSELF.

IN THE YEAR 1810 HE OBTAINED THE RANK OF REAR ADMIRAL,

AND WAS EMPLOYED AT PORTSMOUTH AND GUERNSEY DURING THE REMAINDER OF THE

WAR.

IN APRIL 1833 HE WAS APPOINTED COMMANDER IN CHIEF AT PLYMOUTH

AND REMAINED THERE UNTIL RELIEVED AT THE EXPIRATION OF THE USUAL PERIOD OF

SERVICE IN 1836:

HE SERVED AS LIEUTENANT WITH HIS LATE MAJESTY WILLIAM THE FOURTH

AND WAS AFTERWARDS ALWAYS HONOURED WITH THE GRACIOUS KINDNESS AND

FRIENDSHIP OF THAT MONARCH

NOR SHOULD HIS PRIVATE VIRTUES PASS UNNOTICED.

EXEMPLARY IN CHARACTER IN THE VARIOUS DUTIES OF DOMESTIC AND SOCIAL LIFE

HE WAS BELOVED BY ALL AROUND HIM

KIND AND CONSIDERATE TO THE DISTRESSED HIS BENEVOLENCE ACTIVE AS

UNOSTENTATIOUS

WAS AT ALL TIMES ADMINISTERED WITH CHRISTIAN FEELING

AND HE WILL LONG SURVIVE IN THE MEMORY OF A NUMEROUS CIRCLE OF FRIENDS WHO

KNEW AND VALUED HIM

AND DEEPLY LAMENT THE LOSS THEY HAVE SUSTAINED.

THIS TABLET IS CONSECRATED TO THE MEMORY OF A KIND AND AFFECTIONATE HUSBAND

BY HIS ATTACHED WIFE AND SORROWING WIDOW **MARIA HARGOOD**

DAUGHTER OF **THOMAS SOMERS COCKS, ESQR**

AND GRAND DAUGHTER OF **ALEXANDER THISTLETHWAYTE, OF**

SOUTHWICK PARK, HANTS, ESQR

A.D. 1840.

WILLIAM HARGOOD

had no children. His progress continued: vice admiral, 4 June 1814; KCB, January 1815; GCH (Knight Grand Cross of the Hanoverian Order), 22 March 1831, by the special command of King William whose friendship he still maintained; admiral of the blue, 22 July 1830; GCB, 13 September 1831; commander-in-chief at Plymouth, March 1833 to April 1836; admiral of the white, 10 January 1837. He died at Bath on 12 September 1839 and was buried in Bath Abbey.

SWRH

ELIAB HARVEY
(1758–1830)
Captain HMS *Temeraire*

Perhaps it is only right that the *Temeraire*, so memorably captured in Turner's famous painting, should have had such an equally colourful captain at the time of the great battle in October 1805. Harvey's naval career ended amongst the higher echelons, in spite of an enforced period away from active servicebecause of his maverick character, and his three spells as a parliamentarian. He also had a weakness for serious gambling which, were it not for the compassion of an adversary on one occasion, would have lost him his estate.

Harvey was born on 5 December 1758 at Chigwell in Essex, joined the Royal Navy in 1771 and saw service off North America as a midshipman before promotion to lieutenant in 1779. A brief spell then as a Member of Parliament for Maldon, Essex, preceded his promotion to commander in 1782 and captain the following year.

He continued to serve on both sides of the Atlantic in the *Santa Margarita* and *Valiant*, in the North Sea, twice in the West Indies and with the Channel Fleet, until struck with ill-health in 1797. Conveniently, he was able to take command of Sea Fencibles in 1798 in his native Essex. The next year, he commanded the *Triumph* in which he served in the Channel once more until the Treaty of Amiens in 1802.

Harvey returned to the House of Commons in 1803 as MP for Essex in June 1802. The following year, he was appointed to the *Temeraire*, in which he continued to carry out blockade duties off the west of France until joining Nelson off Cadiz in the autumn of 1805. He left Parliament the same year.

Harvey's Trafalgar started notably. Jockeying for position in the light airs during the long morning approach, the *Temeraire* began to look as if she might overtake the *Victory*. An irritated Nelson hailed across, 'I will thank you, Captain Harvey, to keep your proper station which is astern of the *Victory*.'

In due course, the *Temeraire* cut through the Combined Fleet close astern of Nelson's ship and from then on was in the core of the fight. Following the *Victory*'s example, Harvey's gunners raked the *Bucentaure* as they passed before

Date of death: 20 February 1830

Place of death: Rolls Park, Chigwell, Essex

Where buried: St Andrew's Church, Hempstead, nr Saffron Walden, Essex

OVERVIEW: The north east corner of St Andrews' Church, Hempstead contains a chapel dedicated to the Harvey family, which includes Dr William Harvey, who discovered the circulation of the blood. In the crypt beneath the Harvey chapel it is possible to see the Admiral's coffin. Inside the chapel there is a white marble wall memorial to Admiral Sir Eliab Harvey, and his hatchment hangs on the north wall of the main part of the church.

COFFIN

Location: There are three compartments in the crypt that is entered through a steel trapdoor on the north side of the church beneath the Harvey Chapel. The crypt contains about 50 coffins of members of the Harvey family. The Admiral's coffin, with two others, is in a small bay on the right side.

Description: Made in lead, covered in a velvet draped wooden box with handles, hinges and brass studs. There is a plaque on the top, below the Admiral's coat of arms.

Transcription

SIR ELIAB HARVEY
ADMIRAL OF THE BLUE
Knight Grand Cross of the Bath
(& M.P.)
for…County of Essex
Died 20th Feby 1830
AGED 71 YEARS

going on to engage another five enemy ships. Harvey then attempted to come to the assistance of the *Victory*, which was entangled with the *Redoutable*, although his own ship's rigging was badly damaged. Unavoidably, the *Temeraire* collided with the French ship to sandwich it with the *Victory*. As the *Redoutable*'s demise was hastened, so the three vessels drifted into a fourth, the *Fougueux*, which was sufficiently crippled to permit Harvey's men to take possession of her. Harvey later put the names of his two prizes together to form his personal motto, 'Redoutable et Fougueux'.

Collingwood's report after the battle included a special mention of the brilliant role played by Harvey. His fellow captains felt he had been unfairly singled out but, as result of this 'mention in dispatches', he was showered with formal plaudits from his country, including promotion to rear admiral on 9 November 1805. At Nelson's funeral he was one of the pallbearers.

In 1806 as rear admiral, Harvey joined the *Tonnant* in the Channel Fleet. In 1809, he took issue with his commander, Lord Gambier, about an appointment of Lord Cochrane to command the fireship attack at the Battle of Basque Roads, so vehemently and publicly that he was court-martialled and dismissed the service. Reinstated in 1810 because of his meritorious service record, he was, however, never given an official appointment again. Even so, promotions still came his way, reaching full admiral. He became successively a KCB in 1815 and GCB in 1825.

Harvey served in Parliament again from 1820 until his death at Rools Park, Chigwell, on 20 February 1830. He was buried at Hempstead church.

JRG

HATCHMENT

Location: St Andrew's Church, Hempstead, on the north wall of the main part of the Church.

Description: A diamond-shaped coat of arms, with two shields flanked by Neptune and a unicorn. At the very top is the word 'Temeraire', and below 'Redoutable et Fougueux'.

Transcription

Underneath on a small piece of paper, stuck to the base, is typed the following:

ADMIRAL SIR ELIAB HARVEY G.C.B.
OF ROLLS PARK, CHIGWELL, BORN 5 DEC 1758
DIED 20 FEB 1830. BURIED AT HEMPSTEAD.
HE COMMANDED "FIGHTING TEMERAIRE" AT THE BATTLE OF TRAFALGAR, SUPPORTING SHIP OF LORD NELSON WITH VICTORY IN 1805.

THIS IS THE HATCHMENT AS RESTORED BY SIR FRANCIS WHITMORE, APRIL 1958, AFTER PARTIAL DESTRUCTION SOME 76 YEARS PREVIOUSLY WHEN THE STEEPLE OF HEMPSTEAD CHURCH COLLAPSED AND DESTROYED THE ROOF AND CHANCEL.

WALL MEMORIAL

Description: The inscription is flanked by two columns topped by crocketed pinnacles. Above is an arch containing a coat of arms with Neptune and a unicorn. Above the arms is the word 'Temeraire' and below 'Redoutable et Fougeux'.

Dimensions: Base: 112 cm high x 125 cm wide Memorial: 206 cm high x 125 cm wide

Sculptor: H Hopper, London.

Transcription

TO THE MEMORY OF

ADMIRAL SIR ELIAB HARVEY

KNIGHT GRAND CROSS OF THE BATH, MEMBER OF PARLIAMENT

FOR THIS COUNTY FOR 21 YEARS FROM 1800 TO 1812,

AND FROM 1820 TO 1830;

THIRD SON OF WILLIAM HARVEY, ESQ.

OF ROLLS IN THIS COUNTY,

AND EMMA HIS WIFE, DAUGHTER AND CO-HEIRESS OF

STEPHEN SKINNER, ESQ.

HE WAS BORN ON THE 5TH OF DECEMBER, 1758,

AND DIED AT ROLLS ON THE 20TH OF FEBRUARY 1830.

HE ENTERED THE NAVY IN THE YEAR 1769, AND WAS IN CONSTANT AND

ACTIVE SERVICE IN AMERICA, THE WEST INDIES,

AND THE CHANNEL, FOR 40 YEARS. HE WAS PARTICULARLY

DISTINGUISHED AT THE BATTLE OF TRAFALGAR,

WHERE HE COMMANDED THE TEMERAIRE OF 98 GUNS, WHICH WAS

SELECTED BY LORD NELSON TO BE HIS SUPPORTING SHIP.

HE MARRIED THE LADY LOUISA NUGENT, YOUNGEST DAUGHTER OF

ROBERT EARL NUGENT BY WHOM HE HAD NINE CHILDREN

3 SONS WHO DIED IN HIS LIFE TIME AND 6 DAUGHTERS WHO SURVIVED HIM.

ALSO TO THE MEMORY OF

WILLIAM HARVEY

YOUNGEST SON OF THE ABOVE ADMIRAL SIR E HARVEY, G.C.B.

HE WAS BORN ON THE 23RD OF DECEMBER 1801 AND DIED

ON THE 3RD OF MARCH 1823

WILLIAM HENNAH

(1768–1832)
First Lieutenant HMS *Mars*

Hennah is one of those who had greatness thrust upon him. At approximately the same moment that Lord Nelson received his fatal wound, Captain George Duff of HMS *Mars* (74) was decapitated by a cannon ball fired from the French ship *Fougueux*. Hennah, as first lieutenant, assumed command.

William Hennah was born the son of the Revd Richard Hennah, Vicar of St Austell, Cornwall, and domestic chaplain to Viscount Falmouth. It is recorded that he was baptised on 7 January 1768. The *Gentleman's Magazine* states briefly that 'he entered the Navy under Wallis the circumnavigator.' He was made lieutenant in 1793. Little or nothing appears to be reported of his early career until 17 November 1800, when he first made a name for himself in command of a gallant boat action at Morbihan, in which the French corvette *Réloaise* was boarded and destroyed. As the historian William James remarked, 'The enterprise thus entrusted to Lieutenant Hannah was conducted with great judgement and gallantry.'

On 19 October 1805, HMS *Mars* was the first ship to hoist the signal No 370 – 'The Enemy's ships are coming out of port, or are getting under sail.' On the 21st, she sailed third in Collingwood's column between the *Belleisle* and *Tonnant*. Trying to find an opening in the enemy's line, she was fired upon by the French *Pluton*. To avoid a collision with the Spanish *Santa Ana*, the *Mars* was obliged to turn her head to the wind, thus exposing her stern to the guns of another Spaniard, the *Monarca*, and the French *Algésiras*, which punished her severely until the *Tonnant* was able to come to her aid. The *Mars* with difficulty paid off, only to be further punished by the broadsides of the French *Fougueux*, one of whose shots took off Duff's head.

Hennah fought the *Mars* as well as he was able, given its damaged condition. Including her captain, a total of ninety-eight officers and men were killed or wounded at Trafalgar. For his role at Trafalgar, Hennah received a sword from the Lloyd's Patriotic Fund (the naval gold medal was presented to Duff's widow). On 1 January 1806, he was promoted captain. He also received the unusual honour of a Letter of Commendation from the ship's company. In 1815, he was made a Companion of the Order of the Bath. Marshall merely records he had 'a large family' but at least three of their children were born in Tregony, on the Roseland peninsula, Cornwall.

Captain William Hennah CB died at Tregony on 23 December 1832. *The Times*, in a short obituary, described him as 'one of the old school of British sailors, having entered the Navy under Wallis, the circumnavigator and finished his active career in the wake of Collingwood at Trafalgar.'

AJC

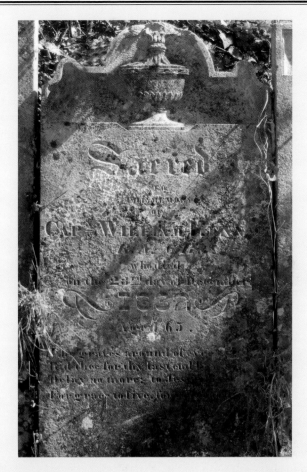

Date of death: 23 December 1832
Place of death: Tregony, Cornwall
Where buried: St Cuby Parish Church,
    Tregony, Cornwall
Description: All headstones were moved in
    the 1960s from their original positions
    and have been relocated around the
    perimeter of the churchyard. The site of
    the grave has been identified as being by
    the wall of the east end of the church.
Dimensions: Headstone: 170 cm x 64 cm.

Transcription

Sacred
TO THE MEMORY OF
CAPN WIILLIAM HENNAH
R.N. C.B.
who died
on the 23rd day of December
1832 Aged 65.

The graves around of every size
Bid thee for thy last end be wise:
Delay no more:- to Jesus fly
For grace to live, for grace to die

George Johnstone Hope

(1767–1818)

Captain HMS *Defence*

Although not one of the 'inner circle' of the Band of Brothers, George Hope nevertheless enjoyed Lord Nelson's confidence and sincere friendship. A portrait of him by Charles Turner, now in the National Portrait Gallery, shows an earnest expression, and, in the way he clutches his telescope, a man devoted to duty.

George Johnstone Hope was born on 6 July 1767. He was the son of the Honourable Charles Hope-Vere, by his third wife, Helen, the daughter of George Dunbar. His grandfather was Charles, First Earl of Hopetoun. He was related also to the Dundas family, a connection that would prove beneficial to his later career.

Young Hope entered the Navy at the age of thirteen on 8 March 1781. He was rated as captain's servant on board HMS *Iphegenia*. On 27 September 1782, he was promoted midshipman. On 29 February 1788, he gained his lieutenancy, and two years later, on 22 November, was made master and commander of the *Racehorse* sloop. He had done well to proceed so far so soon in peacetime.

At the outbreak of war with France in 1793, he was in command of HMS *Bulldog* (13) in the Mediterranean, employed on convoy duty under the command of Vice Admiral Lord Hood. On 13 September the same year, he was promoted captain and given the command of the *Romulus*, serving under Vice Admiral Sir William Hotham. He saw action against the French off Genoa in 1795.

In May 1798, Hope, in the frigate *Alcmene*, was sent by Lord St Vincent to join Nelson in the Mediterranean on his search for the French expeditionary force. Hearing that Nelson's flagship, the *Vanguard*, had been badly damaged in a storm, Hope erroneously supposed that Nelson would make for Gibraltar for repairs and took his ship and the rest of Nelson's frigates there, thus depriving the admiral of his scouts at a critical point on the campaign. 'I thought he would have known me better,' Nelson said in frustration.

Hope continued to serve in the Mediterranean, firstly off Alexandria, where he chased and captured the French gunboat *Légère* and captured dispatches intended for Napoleon, despite a French officer attempting to jettison them. Then he served with Nelson again during the civil war in Naples in 1798/9 when he helped to evacuate the King and Queen of Naples and their entourage from Naples to Palermo. Later, in August 1799, he received a letter from Nelson:

> *I have his Sicilian Majesty's orders to present you in his name a Diamond Ring, as the dispatch states it, 'To Captain Hope, who embarked his Majesty and the Prince Royal in his barge, on the night of December 21st, 1798,' and which his Majesty desires may be accepted by Captain Hope, as a mark of his Royal gratitude. Ever yours, my dear Hope, faithfully and affectionately, Nelson.*

In 1801, he commanded the *Leda* (38) in the Egyptian campaign and continued in active service – so much so that shortly before Trafalgar, it was reported that he had been at home only fourteen months in the previous eight years.

At Trafalgar, HMS *Defence* sailed at the very rear of Collingwood's column, and thus was unable to engage the enemy closely until nearly two and a half hours after firing had commenced. Then, for nearly half an hour, she engaged the French *Berwick*. As that ship pulled away from the *Defence*, only to be attacked by the British *Achilles*, Hope turned his attention to joining the *Revenge* in pounding the Spanish *San Ildefonso* into submission. The *Defence* had thirty-six killed and wounded, and, by comparison with other British ships, suffered relatively minor damage. Hope managed to anchor with his prize and weathered the gale that ensued: as a result, the *San Ildefonso* was one of the few trophies to survive both battle and storm. For the part he played, Hope received the naval gold medal, the thanks of Parliament, and a sword of honour from the Lloyd's Patriotic Fund.

Post Trafalgar, he served in the fleet in the Baltic under Sir James Saumarez, and was made a rear admiral in 1811. In 1812/3 he was sent to bring the Russian fleet to England during the French invasion of that country. When Lord Melville returned to the Admiralty, Hope was again named one of the Lords. His patent is dated 24 May 1816. He continued in this office until his death (which took place at the Admiralty) in May 1818. He was a Knight Commander of the Bath, and for some time MP for East Grinstead.

AJC

Date of death: 2 May 1818
Place of death: The Admiralty
Where buried: Westminster Abbey, London, in the NW tower chapel, west wall, north side.
Description: Wall monument made of white marble, consisting of a pyramid, with a coat of arms at the top, and below naval trophies, flags, coils of rope and cannon balls. The inscription is mounted on two brackets with lion heads.
Sculptor: Peter Turnerelli
Dimensions: 254 cm x 137 cm

Transcription

SACRED TO THE MEMORY OF
REAR ADMIRAL SIR GEORGE HOPE K.C.B.
ERECTED BY SEVERAL CAPTAINS OF THE ROYAL NAVY
WHO SERVED UNDER HIM AS MIDSHIPMEN

Note: Erected 1820 at a cost of £150.
The Admiral was in fact buried a little distance away in the middle aisle of the nave on 9 May 1818, but his actual grave is now covered by the later brass to Sir George Gilbert Scott.

RICHARD KING

(1774–1834)
Captain HMS *Achilles*

The son of an admiral, King was also married to the daughter of Rear Admiral Sir John Duckworth KB, who adopted a protective stance towards his son-in-law. A month before Trafalgar, Duckworth entreated Nelson to take King's ship *Achilles* under his Lordship's command and so King duly joined Nelson's fleet off Cadiz.

Born on 28 November 1774, he entered the Navy in 1788 and was made a post captain before he was twenty – like Nelson, he benefited from influential patrons. In 1797, King sat on the court-martial of Richard Parker who was primarily responsible for the mutiny at the Nore. From that year until 1802, he experienced much action as captain of the frigate *Sirius* (36). He captured two Dutch ships in October 1798 and shortly after claimed a six-gun French vessel and a Spanish brig as prizes. In 1801, in company with a sister ship, he captured a French frigate.

At Trafalgar, the *Achilles* was the seventh ship in Collingwood's line and his first skirmish was squaring up to the *Montanez*, but his challenge was rejected. King went then to the assistance of the *Belleisle*, under fire from three enemy ships. Before doing so, however, he was obliged to engage the *Argonauta*, and the fierce encounter that followed inflicted heavy damage on both sides. After an hour, the Spanish ship broke off in an effort to sail clear and thwarted King's attempt to assemble a boarding party. As the *Achilles* attempted to follow her, she was prevented from doing so by two French ships, *L'Achille* which passed on one side, and the *Berwick* on the other. King and his crew now engaged the *Berwick* in a further hour of intense firing, which ended with the *Achilles* forcing her opponent to strike her colours. In spite of such murderous activity, King, whose ship had barely any superstructure remaining, would report only thirteen killed and fifty-nine wounded amongst his spent crew. A grateful government awarded him the naval gold medal and he also a received a sword of honour from the Lloyd's Patriotic Fund.

Back on station in 1806, Captain King was involved in the capture of four French frigates off Rochefort when Commodore Sir Samuel Hood lost an arm. That year, he succeeded to the baronetcy of his father and then served in the Mediterranean, first as captain of the fleet to Sir Charles Cotton and then, following his promotion to rear admiral in 1812, as second-in-command to Sir Edward Pellew. In January 1815, he was made a Knight Commander of the Bath. Service promotions continued and he was made commander-in-chief in the East Indies in 1816. He became a vice admiral of the red three years later and took command at the Nore in 1833 before dying of cholera, whilst still serving, on 5 August 1834 in Sheerness.

JRG

Date of death: 5 August 1834
Place of death: Admiralty House, Sheerness
Where buried: All Saints Church, Eastchurch,
Isle of Sheppey
Description: Wall monument made of white
marble mounted on black, consisting of a
pyramid formed of sails and the prow of a
ship, a cannon and cannon balls. Below is
a coat of arms with two shields and the
mottos 'Tria juncta in uno' and 'Jamais
sans esperance'
Sculptor: C Thompson, Osnaburgh St,
Regents Park, London
Dimensions: 300 cm x 110 cm
Note: The Admiral was buried under the
floor in the centre of the chancel, but this
is unmarked.

Transcription

SACRED TO THE MEMORY OF
VICE ADMIRAL **SIR RICHARD KING** BARONET K.C.B.
COMMANDER IN CHIEF AT THE NORE
WHO DIED OF AN ATTACK OF CHOLERA MORBUS AT THE ADMIRALTY HOUSE SHEERNESS
ON THE 5TH OF AUGUST 1834, AGED 61 YEARS.

HE DISTINGUISHED HIMSELF IN THE NORTH SEAS AS CAPTAIN OF THE SIRIUS FRIGATE
COMMANDED THE ACHILLE, 74 GUNS, AT THE BATTLE OF TRAFALGAR
AND, IN 1816, WAS APPOINTED COMMANDER IN CHIEF IN THE EAST INDIES.

HE WAS TWICE MARRIED,
FIRST, A.D.1803, TO ANNE SARAH, DAUGHTER OF
ADMIRAL SIR JOHN DUCKWORTH BART G.C.B. OF WEAR HOUSE, DEVONSHIRE,
BY WHOM HE HAD FOUR SONS AND ONE DAUGHTER.
SECONDLY, A.D.1822, TO MARIA SUSANNA, DAUGHTER OF
ADMIRAL SIR CHARLES COTTON BART OF LANWADE, CAMBRIDGESHIRE,
BY WHOM HE HAD FOUR SONS AND THREE DAUGHTERS.

HIS WIFE AND TWELVE CHILDREN, SURVIVE TO DEPLORE THE LOSS OF
A TENDER HUSBAND AND AFFECTIONATE FATHER.
HIS NUMEROUS RELATIVES, AND FRIENDS, AND ATTACHED FOLLOWERS,
EVINCE BY THEIR GRIEF
THE LOVE AND RESPECT WHICH HE INSPIRED

FRANCIS LAFOREY

(1767–1835)

Captain HMS *Spartiate*

An American, Laforey was born in Virginia in 1767 to influential parents. His father, Admiral Sir John Laforey (1729–96) was descended from a Huguenot family that came to Britain in the company of William III in 1688, and was a baronet in his own right. Lady Laforey's father was a member of the Council at Antigua, and so the careers of both John and Francis were closely linked to the West Indies.

So, for example, in 1791, under the orders of his father, Francis, then aged twenty-four, was in command of the *Fairy* sloop on the Leeward Island station. The first action taken by Sir John Laforey when news of the war with France arrived in Antigua, in 1793, was to mount an attack upon the island of Tobago, and then to send his son to England with the dispatches of his success. As a result, four days after arriving in London, Francis was made post captain – the usual reward for those bringing victory dispatches. Laforey was soon appointed to the *Carysfort*, a 34-gun frigate with a crew of 197 men. On 29 May 1794, she fell in with the *Castor*, a French frigate that had been formerly a British frigate of that name commanded by Sir Thomas Troubridge and captured when Admiral Nielly's squadron overtook a large convoy that the *Castor* was shepherding to England from Newfoundland.

The action took just over an hour and whereas the *Carysfort* suffered one man killed and a few wounded and very little damage to their ship, the French were left with sixteen dead and nine wounded. James points out that Laforey had under him an entirely new crew and that the French were faced with fighting a ship rigged English-fashion, where every line and sail were new to them, so it must have been a somewhat confused fight.

In 1795, Captain Laforey was given command of *L'Aimable* (32), a fine French frigate, and in her transported his father back to Antigua where Sir John resumed his appointment as commander-in-chief of the Leeward Islands. Early the next year, Laforey took command of the *Scipio* (64) and under the orders of Commodore Parr, assisted in the capture of the Dutch islands of Demerara, Essiquibo and Berbice.

In 1796, Sir John was relieved of his command of the Leeward Islands, and on his return journey to England, succumbed to yellow fever. In 1797, Francis succeeded to the baronetcy and took command of the *Hydra* frigate and cruised off the French coast. In 1799 and 1800, the *Hydra* was employed in the Leeward Islands and upon Sir Francis's return to England, he was given the command of HMS *Powerful* (74) and was ordered to the Baltic and then to Gibraltar and, lastly, to the West Indies.

With the renewal of the war in 1803, Laforey was given command of the *Spartiate* (74), and was in the West Indies when Nelson's squadron arrived there

Date of death: 17 June 1835
Place of death: Brighton
Where buried: St Nicholas Church, Brighton
Note: Records show that Sir Francis Laforey Bt KCB, of Grand Parade, Brighton, aged 67 years, was buried at St Nicholas Church on 24 June 1835 (E Sussex Record Office ref PAR 255/1/5/5). The Brighton Corporation Act 1931 included powers to remove any tombstone or monument in order to better drain, level, lay out, plant, ornament or otherwise improve disused burial grounds. Some of the tombstones of St Nicholas were moved in the late 1940s/early 1950s, and a transcript made of them, but there is no record that Sir Francis's stone was among them. The graveyard has now been almost completely cleared and all flat headstones have been placed around the edge of the site. However, very few are readable, perhaps because the church is situated high up above the town and would have been subject to sea gales corroding the stones. Therefore it must be concluded that there now remains no visible record on the ground of the grave.

in June 1805, in pursuit of the combined squadrons of France and Spain. The *Spartiate* then joined Nelson's squadron for the return to Europe and, ultimately, the Battle of Trafalgar.

The 21 October was a frustrating day for him, since his ship was the last ship in Nelson's line. With light wind, it took most of the afternoon for the *Spartiate* and *Minotaur* to get into action, but when they did, they had their moment. Bearing down upon these two British 74s were five ships of the combined fleet's van under Rear Admiral Dumanoir: the *Formidable*, *Duguay-Trouin*, *Scipion*, *Mont Blanc* and *Neptuno*. Captains Laforey and Mansfield, of the *Minotaur*, poured broadside after broadside into the leading ship *Formidable*. Faced with this, Dumanoir avoided action with three of his ships following him, but leaving the Spanish *Neptuno* (84) to face the two British 74s alone. After an hour it was all over and the *Spartiate*'s losses were three killed and twenty wounded.

Following Trafalgar, the *Spartiate* returned to England and Sir Francis participated in Lord Nelson's funeral as the bearer of the Standard. He stayed with the *Spartiate* and was employed in the Mediterranean until 1810 when he was advanced to rear admiral. His first appointment as an admiral was as commander-in-chief of the Leeward Islands, where he remained until 1814. Returning to England, he never saw active service again, although he advanced up the ranks to full admiral, and died in Brighton in 1835.

SCC

'*Trafalgar – the end of the day*', engraving after Nicholas Pocock. Spartiate *can be seen engaging* Neptuno *on the horizon.*

John Richards Lapenotiere

(1770–1834)
Lieutenant commanding HM Schooner *Pickle*

As a lieutenant, Lapenotiere was responsible in 1805 for delivering to the Admiralty in London the news of both the victory of Trafalgar and the death of Nelson.

Off Cape Trafalgar on 26 October, five days after the battle, Collingwood entrusted his Trafalgar dispatch to Lapenotiere, who commanded HM Schooner *Pickle*, with orders to deliver it to the Admiralty in London. The task was given by Collingwood to Lapenotiere in recognition of his initiative some years earlier in preventing a ship in which they were both passengers from foundering.

On reaching the western approaches to the English Channel on 1 November, Lapenotiere was prevented by adverse winds from progressing further up Channel. He therefore put into Falmouth and landed with the dispatch at noon on 4 November, organised transport to London by post chaise, and arrived at the Admiralty in Whitehall at 1am on 6 November after a continuous 271-mile journey of thirty-six hours, including twenty-one changes of horses. He delivered the dispatch to William Marsden, Secretary to the Navy, who promptly alerted Lord Barham, First Lord of the Admiralty. Copies of the dispatch were then made and delivered to William Pitt, Prime Minister, at 3am, to the King, who was at Windsor, and other key figures in London.

Lapenotiere received promotion to commander and a £500 gratuity for his achievement and was subsequently awarded a 100-guinea sword by the Lloyd's Patriotic Fund. King George III also presented him with a silver sugar sifter (now in Liskeard Museum in Cornwall).

John Richards Lapenotiere was a member of an old Huguenot family that had settled in Devon and had had a continuous record of military service to the Crown. He first went to sea at the age of ten in the armed ship *Three Sisters*, under the protection of his father. Then in 1785, as a gentleman volunteer at the age of fifteen, he joined a commercial expedition under Lieutenant Nathaniel

Portlock, who had previously sailed with Captain James Cook, to exploit the potential in the fur trade on the north-west coast of America. After returning to England in 1788, he then served successively as a midshipman in the sloop *Scout* (14) and the *Magnificent* (74). Then, in 1791, at the age of twenty-one, he joined the merchant ship *Assistance*, again commanded by Nathaniel Portlock, as an able seaman. The *Assistance* sailed as a tender to Captain William Bligh's ship, the *Providence* (12), in his second breadfruit expedition to the Pacific, the first having been frustrated by the mutiny in the *Bounty*.

Shortly after returning to England in 1793, Lapenotiere joined the *Margarita* (38), part of the British West Indies fleet commanded by Vice Admiral Sir John Jervis. He then transferred briefly to Jervis's flagship, the *Boyne* (98), before being promoted lieutenant and appointed to the command of the schooner *Berbice* (16). Then, in 1795, he returned to England as first lieutenant in the *Resource* (40).

In 1800, after serving uneventfully in a frigate and three ships of the line in the North Sea and Channel fleets, he was appointed to the command of the hired cutter *Joseph*. He engaged in several successful actions to disrupt French coastal shipping near Brest, earning himself the written approbation of the commander-in-chief, Earl St Vincent.

Shortly after the *Joseph* was paid off in 1802, he was appointed to the command of the *Pickle* (10), a Bermuda-built schooner that had been bought into the Royal Navy in the West Indies. In the *Pickle*, he earned great approval in 1804 for his efforts in saving the crew of the *Magnificent* (74), in which he had five years earlier served as midshipman, when she was wrecked near Brest. And later, when attached to Nelson's fleet prior to Trafalgar, he captured a Portuguese ship with a cargo of bullocks, which he sent on to the fleet for replenishment of their supplies of fresh meat.

After his promotion to commander following the delivery of the Trafalgar dispatch, Lapenotiere briefly commanded the armed ship *Chapman* (16), based in Scotland, before joining his last command, the brig *Orestes* (16), in late 1806. The *Orestes* served on the North Sea station until 1807, when she joined the fleet of Admiral Gambier bound for Copenhagen. Off Elsinore, he was injured and badly burnt by a flash-back from one of the guns, but continued in command of the ship, which was transferred to the Plymouth station. From here he captured a letter of marque, *La Conception,* an American merchantman and the *Loup Garou* (16), a newly-built French privateer.

Lapenotiere was discharged from the *Orestes* in 1811 and made post captain. He had no further service at sea. He had married Lucia Shean in 1800, by whom he had four daughters. After Lucia's death in 1804, he married in 1805 Mary Anne Graves, by whom he had four daughters and three sons, two of whom also served in the Royal Navy. He settled in the hamlet of Roseland, at Menheniot, near Liskeard, Cornwall. He died in 1834 and is buried in Menheniot church-yard with his second wife, who predeceased him, and his third son, Thomas.

GWW

Date of death: 19 January 1834
Place of death: Menheniot, Cornwall (his house still stands within the parish at Roseland).
Where buried: Menheniot Parish Church, on north side of the churchyard.
Description: A brick tomb, topped by a black slate slab on which lies a flat limestone slab with an inscription.
Dimensions: 157 cm x 80 cm x 58 cm high.

Transcription

SACRED TO THE MEMORY OF
M A LAPENOTIERE
WIFE OF
CAPTAIN JOHN RICHARDS LAPENOTIERE
WHO DEPARTED THIS LIFE
THE 1[?] OF JULY 1833
AGED 55

ALSO
OF JOHN RICHARDS LAPENOTIERE
HER HUSBAND
WHO DEPARTED THIS LIFE
THE 19TH JANUARY 1834
AGED 63 YEARS

ALSO OF THOMAS
YOUNGEST SON OF THE ABOVE
WHO DIED NOVEMBER 12TH
1876 AGED 64

Charles John Moore Mansfield
(1760–1813)
Captain HMS *Minotaur*

Little personal information is known about Mansfield, but a good deal is known about the ships in which he served, and their record almost summarises the wars against Revolutionary America and France.

Mansfield's exact date of birth is still unknown, but we know that he was christened on 13 December 1760 at Stoke Damerel, Devon, and was commissioned lieutenant on 25 November 1778.

Joining HMS *Albion* as fifth lieutenant in 1779, he took part in four actions in that ship. In a fleet of twenty-six of the line under Vice Admiral the Hon John Byron (*Princess Royal*), he fought Vice Admiral Comte d'Estaing off Grenada on 6 July 1779. Four dismasted British ships escaped, 'the French admiral's seamanship not being equal to his courage.' He was then in a squadron of eight liners under Hyde Parker (also *Princess Royal*) that captured nine sail of a French convoy, burned ten others and engaged the escort off Fort Royal, Martinique, on 18 December 1779. Under Rodney (*Sandwich*), he took part in two inconclusive engagements against Vice Admiral Comte de Guichen, thirty miles west-south-west of the north of Martinique, on 17 April 1780, and twenty miles east of the island on 15 May 1780.

An opportunity then arose to gain greater experience of seniority in a smaller ship, and in 1781 he became first lieutenant of the frigate HMS *Fortunée*, a French prize captured on 21 December 1779 by HMS *Suffolk* north-west of St Lucia. The date of his transfer to the *Fortunée* is uncertain but he may well have participated in the extremely disappointing encounter twelve miles north-east of Cape Henry, Virginia, between Rear Admiral Thomas Graves and Vice Admiral Comte de Grasse, on 5 September 1781, that was partly responsible for the fall of Yorktown.

His next appointment, in 1783, was as third lieutenant in HMS *Irresistible*, followed in the same year by the first lieutenancy in HMS *Monsieur*, a former French privateer captured in 1780. After 1783, with the end of the War of American Independence, he seems to have had a 'career break': his next appointment was not until 1790, when in the Revolutionary War with France he was made first lieutenant of HMS *Lion*. What happened in the intervening years? Did he marry and have children? He was of an age to do so, but at present we do not know.

From the *Lion* he moved in 1792 to HMS *Assistance*, again as first lieutenant, a role that he discharged for the last time on his transfer to HMS *Stately* in 1793. On 19 July that year, he was promoted commander and moved to the sloop HMS *Megaera*, as her commanding officer: while still in the *Megaera*, he jumped the great hurdle in every naval officer's life and was 'made post' on 4 October 1794.

In 1795, his first command as post captain was the frigate HMS *Sphinx*,

Date of death: 23 April 1813

Place of death: ? Rochester

Where buried: St Margaret's Church, Rochester, Kent

Description: Wall monument situated some 274 cm up on the north wall of the gallery of the Church. It consists of, at the top, an urn in relief against a black marble background. The main body is in white marble with black lettering, and there is a coat of arms at the base, in blue and white.

Dimensions: 190 cm x 80 cm

Transcription

TO THE MEMORY OF
Captⁿ CHARLES JOHN MOORE MANSFIELD
ROYAL NAVY

Who during a Period of forty years arduous Service established the
Character of an Honorable, and Gallant Officer.
In the Year 1792 he was made Commander and soon afterwards
raised to the Rank of
POST CAPTAIN.
While commanding the Andromache he was attacked by an Algerine Frigate
under Spanish Colors, which he captured after
a long and desperate engagement.
For many years he commanded the Minotaur, and had the Honor of
capturing the El Neptuno, a Spanish 80 Gun Ship,
in the ever memorable Engagement of
TRAFALGAR.
Soon after this Period, worn down by fatigue, he retired into the bosom
of his Family, and, after a long and afflicting Illness,
calmly resigned his Soul into the hands of his Maker
on the 23^{d.} day of April 1813. Aged 52 Years.

followed later that year by another frigate, HMS *Andromache* (32), in which he quite easily captured an aggressive *Algerine* (24) corsair on 30 January 1797, which had apparently misjudged the British warship as a Portuguese. The *Algerine* surrendered after the loss of sixty-four killed and forty wounded, against two dead and four wounded in the *Andromache*.

Mansfield's next command was HMS *Dryad*, 1799–1803, followed by HMS *Minotaur*, which had fought with red-painted sides at the Battle of the Nile on 1–2 August 1798. In her command and in company with HM ships *Thunderer* and *Albion*, he chased and captured the French frigate *Franchise* (40) in the Channel on 20 May 1803. Admiral Collingwood was briefly in the *Minotaur* in 1803, while his ship the *Venerable* was away replenishing.

Few of Mansfield's ships were really distinguished while he was present, and if the impression given here of him is that of an able but average officer, not reaching captaincy until his middle thirties, it is an impression reinforced by the *Trafalgar Roll*'s observation that 'of the work of the *Minotaur* in the battle of Trafalgar there is not very much to be said. In company with the *Spartiate* in the weather division, she forced the Spanish *Neptuno* to surrender, losing in the encounter three men killed and twenty-two wounded. Her only damage consisted in her spars being wounded.' For his part, Mansfield received the naval gold medal, the thanks of Parliament, and a sword of honour from the Lloyd's Patriotic Fund – the typical rewards for the British captains present.

He did not cease service after Trafalgar, but the impression of 'able but average' is further strengthened by a tiny personal glimpse given by Collingwood, nearly a year after Trafalgar, in the summer of 1806: 'I am sorry [to] hear poor Mansfield is complaining again of his rheumaticks but I hope he will be in England in the turnip season, which will cure him of all his complaints.' In the *Minotaur*, Mansfield was flag captain to Rear Admiral William Essington, and third-in-command at the second Battle of Copenhagen on 2 September 1807; he died in April 1813. It may be said that from posterity's viewpoint he had two misfortunes: the lack of correspondence and other sources of insight into his personality, leaving him relatively unknowable to us today; and the seeming fact of being an 'able but average' officer in an age when the average in the Royal Navy was so high. In another era, he might have been more distinguished; yet like today, it was on the 'able but average' that so much fundamentally depended.

SWRH

ROBERT MOORSOM

(1760–1835)
Captain HMS *Revenge*

Moorsom's account of the British order of battle is considered amongst the most accurate record of Trafalgar, when he and his ship covered themselves in glory. Interestingly, it is also one of the few accounts of the battle that is openly critical of Nelson's tactics. He wrote, 'I am not certain that our mode of attack was the best.'

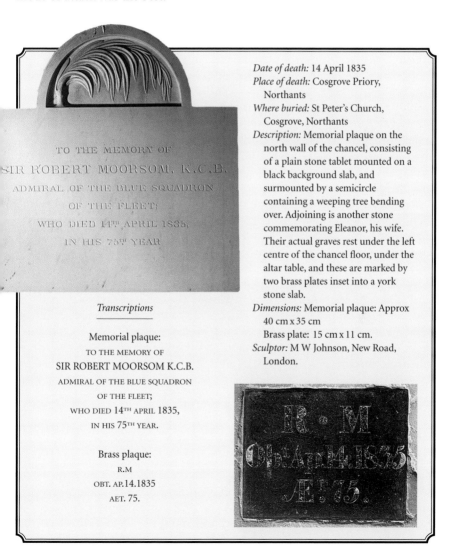

Date of death: 14 April 1835
Place of death: Cosgrove Priory, Northants
Where buried: St Peter's Church, Cosgrove, Northants
Description: Memorial plaque on the north wall of the chancel, consisting of a plain stone tablet mounted on a black background slab, and surmounted by a semicircle containing a weeping tree bending over. Adjoining is another stone commemorating Eleanor, his wife. Their actual graves rest under the left centre of the chancel floor, under the altar table, and these are marked by two brass plates inset into a york stone slab.
Dimensions: Memorial plaque: Approx 40 cm x 35 cm
Brass plate: 15 cm x 11 cm.
Sculptor: M W Johnson, New Road, London.

Transcriptions

Memorial plaque:
TO THE MEMORY OF
SIR ROBERT MOORSOM K.C.B.
ADMIRAL OF THE BLUE SQUADRON
OF THE FLEET;
WHO DIED 14TH APRIL 1835,
IN HIS 75TH YEAR.

Brass plaque:
R.M
OBT. AP.14.1835
AET. 75.

He was born at Whitby, Yorkshire, on 8 June 1760 and entered the Navy at the age of seventeen. As a midshipman he served in the Channel, at Gibraltar, and saw action off Cape Spartel. He also participated in the capture of part of a West Indies bound convoy in 1782. Promotion to lieutenant came two years later and he was a captain by 1790. Passing through the command of four ships, he took over the newly-built *Revenge*, in time to see service at the blockade of Cadiz under Collingwood and then at the Battle of Trafalgar.

During the initial approach to battle on 21 October 1805, Moorsom's ship lay eighth in line in Collingwood's column, with the objective to attack Vice Admiral Gravina's flagship, the *Principe de Asturias*. However, the *Revenge*'s turn of speed brought her ahead of two others, thereby being able to open fire first at the *San Ildefonso*. Shortly afterwards, Moorsom turned his attention to the French *Achille*, and within a quarter of an hour had downed two of her masts. The *Revenge* then took on the *Aigle*, close enough to foul her jib boom and administer two broadsides before eventually setting about 'my friend the Spanish Admiral', as Moorsom afterwards wrote. She was the first to engage the *Principe de Asturias,* and the powerful three-decker, together with the support of three other enemy ships, was able to inflict severe punishment on Moorsom's ship, wounding him in the process. However, relief came in the form of the *Dreadnought* and *Thunderer*, and not before time as the *Revenge* was badly holed below the waterline.

Returning home to recover from his wounds, Moorsom featured prominently at Nelson's funeral, carrying the Great Banner during the ceremonies. His own heroic role was also formally recognised by the government, in addition to being presented with the naval gold metal and a sword of honour from the Lloyd's Patriotic Fund.

He was appointed rear admiral in 1810, vice admiral in 1814 and served as a Lord of the Admiralty during 1809/10. He was a Member of Parliament and was made a Knight Commander of the Bath in 1815. Other appointments included being made a colonel of Marines and Master General of the Ordnance. He died as an admiral of the blue on 14 April 1835 at Cosgrove Priory, Northamptonshire.

JRG

JAMES NICOLL MORRIS
(1763–1830)
Captain HMS *Colossus*

James Nicoll Morris was born in 1763, the son of Captain John Morris RN. When his father was killed in command of HMS *Bristol* at the unsuccessful attack on Sullivan's Island, Charlestown, in 1776 during the War of American Independence, James, aged thirteen, had been in the service for nearly one year. His father, like Nelson, left his progeny to King and Country.

Prior to Trafalgar, his naval career was relatively uneventful. In 1779, he was in the *Prince of Wales* at the actions of St Lucia and Grenada and was promoted lieutenant a year later. In 1793, on the Newfoundland station, his sloop *Plato* took part in the capture of the French *Lutine*. In the same year, he was promoted captain. Five years later, his frigate *Lively* was lost on Rota Point, near Cadiz, and a year later he conducted Lord Elgin to Constantinople in the *Phaeton*, staying in the Mediterranean to co-operate with the Austrians.

During 1804/5, he commanded the *Colossus* (74), 'an excellent sailer' according to Collingwood, and took part in the blockade of Brest and the watch off Cadiz. When he first assumed command, she was a sickly ship with an unpromising crew, but by October 1805 he had transformed her into a formidable fighting vessel. She gave a good account of herself at Trafalgar where she was the sixth ship of Cuthbert Collingwood's somewhat ragged division. Once engaged, Morris's ship suffered from heavy fire from the French *Swiftsure* and *Argonaute*. The latter collided with the *Colossus* and sandwiched her between the two enemy ships. She endured a furious and heavy punishment from their great guns. Even though the *Colossus*'s carronades were able to clear the enemy upper decks of men, the *Argonaute*'s crew prepared to board but were prevented from doing so when the two ships were driven apart by the swell. Morris next engaged the *Bahama* and was able to bring down her mizzen mast, before being supported by Codrington in the *Orion*.

At the end of the battle, Morris was able to share in a success that had accounted for three of the enemy ships. However, the *Colossus* had suffered the highest casualties of any of the British ships: forty killed and 160 wounded. Morris was among them. He was hit in the knee. The pain was great, but he applied his own tourniquet to stop the bleeding and refused to leave the quarterdeck. Nevertheless, at the close of the action, he fainted from loss of blood and was finally carried below. He recovered in Gibraltar and subsequently received the thanks of Parliament, the naval gold medal and a vase from the Lloyd's Patriotic Fund for his part in the battle (see illustration on page 125).

In 1810, Morris was appointed a colonel of Marines and in 1811, was raised to rear admiral. In 1812, he was third in command in the Baltic and in 1815, he was made KCB. His last promotion was to vice admiral. Morris died in Marlow on 15 April 1830. His wife, whom he had married in 1802, wrote of him that his 'strict sense of honour rendered him universally respected and esteemed,' and that he was 'distinguished in simplicity and singleness of heart for which he was remarkable.'

PW

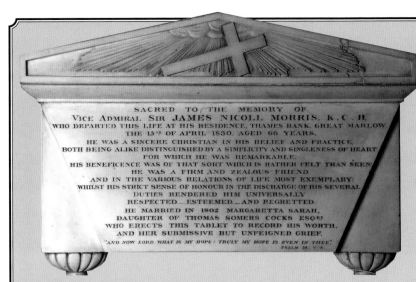

Date of death: 15 April 1830

Place of death: Thames Bank, Great Marlow, Bucks

Where buried: All Saints Church, Marlow, Bucks

Description: White marble tablet on the south wall in the Lady Chapel adjacent to the rood screen. The inscription is surmounted by an archetrave consisting of a diagonally-placed cross on a background of rays of light. The search for the grave has been unsuccessful, perhaps because many headstones in the graveyard are badly weathered.

Dimensions: 93 cm x 61 cm.

Transcription

SACRED TO THE MEMORY OF

VICE ADMIRAL **SIR JAMES NICOLL MORRIS**, K.C.B.

WHO DEPARTED THIS LIFE AT HIS RESIDENCE, THAMES BANK, GREAT MARLOW

THE 15TH OF APRIL 1830, AGED 66 YEARS.

HE WAS A SINCERE CHRISTIAN IN HIS BELIEF AND PRACTICE,

BOTH BEING ALIKE DISTINGUISHED BY A SIMPLICITY AND SINGLENESS OF HEART

FOR WHICH HE WAS REMARKABLE.

HIS BENEFICENCE WAS OF THAT SORT WHICH IS RATHER FELT THAN SEEN

HE WAS A FIRM AND ZEALOUS FRIEND

AND IN THE VARIOUS RELATIONS OF LIFE MOST EXEMPLARY

WHILST HIS STRICT SENSE OF HONOUR IN THE DISCHARGE OF HIS SEVERAL

DUTIES RENDERED HIM UNIVERSALLY

RESPECTED - ESTEEMED - AND REGRETTED.

HE MARRIED IN 1802 MARGARETTA SARAH,

DAUGHTER OF THOMAS SOMERS COCKS ESQRE

WHO ERECTS THIS TABLET TO RECORD HIS WORTH

AND HER SUBMISSIVE BUT UNFEIGNED GRIEF.

AND NOW LORD WHAT IS ONLY HOPE: TRULY MY HOPE IS EVEN IN THEE.

PSALM 39 V6

HORATIO, LORD NELSON

Date of death: 21 October 1805
Place of death: Trafalgar
Where buried: The crypt of St Paul's Cathedral, London
Description: A black marble sarcophagus, surmounted by a gilded viscount's coronet placed on a red cushion. It stands on a rectangular black base with white decoration, on the south side of which is inscribed in gold the words: HORATIO.VISC.NELSON

The whole stands on a large rectangular stone base, inside which the coffin is laid.
Sculptor: Benedetto da Rovezzano (who originally created the sarcophagus for Cardinal Wolsey).
Dimensions: Base: 320 cm x 219 cm. Height: 320 cm.

Transcription

None apart from the above

MARBLE STATUE

Location: South transept, St Paul's Cathedral, London

Description: A large marble statue of Nelson in the undress uniform of a vice admiral, with four orders on his left breast and two medals round his neck. His Turkish 'pelisse' is draped over his right shoulder and his left hand rests on an anchor and coil of cable. The statue stands on a plinth bearing the names of his battles: COPENHAGEN, NILE, TRAFALGAR, and a bas relief of three reclining sea gods. On the left side Britannia points out Nelson to two boys dressed as midshipmen, and on the right is a mourning lion.

Sculptor: John Flaxman

Transcription

ERECTED AT THE PUBLIC EXPENSE
TO THE MEMORY OF
VICE-ADMIRAL HORATIO, VISCOUNT NELSON, K.B.
TO RECORD HIS SPLENDID AND UNPARALLELLED ACHIEVEMENTS,
DURING A LIFE SPENT IN THE SERVICE OF HIS COUNTRY,
AND TERMINATED IN THE MOMENT OF VICTORY BY A GLORIOUS DEATH,
IN THE MEMORABLE ACTION OFF CAPE TRAFALGAR ON THE XXI OF OCTOBER MDCCCV.
LORD NELSON WAS BORN ON THE XXIX OF SEPTEMBER MDCCLVIII.
THE BATTLE OF THE NILE WAS FOUGHT ON THE 1 OF AUGUST MDCCXCVIII,
THE BATTLE OF COPENHAGEN ON THE II OF APRIL MDCCCI.

Nelson has been memorialised in many ways and in many different locations. For a full list of all the monuments to him, and the story behind their design and erection, see, Flora Fraser, 'If you seek his monument' in C. White, The Nelson Companion (Sutton Publishing 1995, new edition 2005)

WILLIAM CARNEGIE, EARL OF NORTHESK

(1756–1831)
Rear Admiral and third-in-command HMS *Britannia*

Although third-in-command at Trafalgar, Northesk played very little part in the battle, or in the planning that preceded it. He and Nelson had not served together before – although Nelson, as was his custom, made a point of getting to know his new subordinate, and of winning his confidence. He dined with him privately on at least two occasions in the weeks before the battle and consulted him on the appointment of officers to the *Britannia*.

Northesk was born in Hampshire on 10 April 1756. His father, the sixth earl, had also served in the Royal Navy and so the young William went to sea in 1771, the same year as Nelson. He served as a lieutenant in Admiral Sir George Rodney's flagship, HMS *Sandwich*, at the victory over the French on 17 April 1780, and was promoted commander for his part in the battle. He reached post rank in April 1782 and commanded the frigate HMS *Enterprise*. Ten years later, he succeeded to the earldom.

During the war against Revolutionary France, he commanded frigates until his appointment to the *Monmouth* (64), an East Indiaman converted on the stocks, in 1796. He was still in command when his ship's company was involved in the Mutiny at the Nore, in 1797. Having been imprisoned on board for a while, he was then asked by the delegates to take their demands to the King, which he agreed to do. When the demands were rejected, he remained in London and resigned his command.

In 1803, he was appointed to command the First Rate battleship *Britannia* in the Channel Fleet and when he was promoted rear admiral in April 1804, he remained in her. He was part of a detachment sent south under Sir Robert Calder in August 1805 to assist in blockading the Combined Fleet in Cadiz.

At Trafalgar, the *Britannia* was in Nelson's line and was hotly engaged with a number of enemy ships, including the *Santissima Trinidad*, suffering fifty-two casualties. Northesk was made a Knight of the Bath and was given the naval gold medal, the freedom of the City of London and a vase worth £300 from the Lloyd's Patriotic Fund.

He did not serve at sea again, although he was created rear admiral of the United Kingdom in 1821 and served as commander-in-chief at Plymouth during 1827–30. He died in Albemarle Street, London, on 28 May 1831 and was buried in St Paul's Cathedral alongside Nelson and Collingwood.

CSW

Date of death: 28 May 1831
Place of death: Albemarle St, London
Where buried: The crypt (north side) of St Paul's Cathedral, London
Description: A plain box tomb, made of stone, with a brass plaque bearing the inscription.
Dimensions: 230 cm x 93 cm x 71.5 cm high

Transcription

(in Gothic lettering)

Sacred to the Memory of William vii. Earl
of Northesk G.C.B.Admiral of the Red
Rear Admiral of Great Britain and third in
command in the glorious Victory of Trafalgar.
Born April x MDCClviii
Died May xxviii MDCCCxxxi

ISRAEL PELLEW

(1758–1832)

Captain HMS *Conqueror*

Pellew spent all his career in the shadow of his more dashing elder brother, the famous frigate captain Edward Pellew, and even at Trafalgar he was not able to escape from his reputation. His ship, HMS *Conqueror*, arrived in the thick of the fighting just as Villeneuve, in the *Bucentaure*, surrendered. Pellew sent his captain of Marines, James Atcherly, in a boat to receive the French admiral's submission. 'It is a satisfaction to me that it is to so fortunate an officer as Sir Edward Pellew that I have surrendered,' remarked the courteous Villeneuve. 'It is his brother, sir,' replied an embarrassed Atcherly. 'His brother! What, are there two of them? Helas!'

The third son of Samuel Humphrey Pellew, Israel was born on 25 August 1758 and went to sea in 1771, becoming a lieutenant in 1779. He was promoted commander in 1790 and served with his elder brother in the frigate HMS *Nymphe* when she captured the French *Cléopâtre* on 18 June 1793. For his part in this action, he was made a post captain.

He then had a rapid series of commands, before finally being appointed to the fine new battleship HMS *Conqueror* (74) in April 1804, succeeding one of Nelson's closest professional friends, Thomas Louis, as her captain. In her, he joined Nelson in the Mediterranean in September 1804 and took part in every stage of the Trafalgar campaign, including the chase to the West Indies and back in the summer of 1805.

At Trafalgar, the *Conqueror* was fifth in Nelson's line and Pellew first positioned her off the *Bucentaure*'s quarter, forcing the already badly-damaged French flagship to surrender. Not wishing to waste time with the formal ceremony, Pellew sent Atcherly to receive Villeneuve's sword, and moved on to assist the *Neptune* in her attack on the massive *Santissima Trinidad*. When she, in turn, surrendered, Pellew moved on once more and took part in the attack on the French ship *L'Intrepide* under Captain Infernet. Pellew and his men had thus contributed to the capture of three enemy ships – a record matched by few others in the British fleet. Pellew himself had been thrown to the deck and momentarily stunned by the wind of a passing shot and, although he quickly recovered, he discovered later that he had received a permanent injury.

However, he did not report himself wounded and so did not appear on the official casualty list.

After the battle, Pellew attempted to take the *Bucentaure* in tow, putting a party of sailors on board under the command of Lieutenant Richard Spear – they were captured when the French ship went ashore off Cadiz in the great storm that followed the battle. Pellew received the naval gold medal and a sword from the Lloyd's Patriotic Fund, and the *Conqueror* received a new figurehead. The head of her old one had been shot away and the crew petitioned that it should be replaced with a bust of Nelson, which was duly done in Plymouth Dockyard. Pellew continued in command of her until 1808, stationed off Cadiz and Lisbon.

Promoted rear admiral in 1810, he served in the Mediterranean as captain of the fleet when his elder brother became commander-in-chief, but he never commanded a fleet in his own right and did not serve at sea again after 1816. He was created KCB in 1815 and reached the rank of full admiral in 1830. He died on 19 July 1832 and was buried at Charles Church, in Plymouth.

CSW

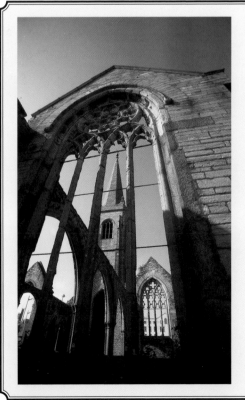

Date of death: 19 July 1832
Place of death: Ham Street, Plymouth
Where buried: Charles the Martyr Church, Plymouth
Note: Records show that Sir Israel Pellew K.C.B. was buried at Charles Church, Pymouth on 26 July 1832 (Burial Register in Plymouth & West Devon Record Office). On the night of 21 March 1941 the church was gutted by fire in one of the heaviest air raids on Plymouth of WW2. It remained in a derelict state until 1957 when it was decided it would not be rebuilt. The ruins still stand as a memorial, but the graveyard has now gone, and the remains buried there were removed and re-interred at Efford Cemetery. However there is no record of Sir Israel Pellew's remains being included among those which were removed.
Therefore it must be concluded that there now remains no visible record on the ground of the grave.

JOHN PILFOLD

(1768–1834)

Acting Captain HMS *Ajax*

Long-standing confusion over the date of Pilfold's birth may be clarified here: although the precise date remains unknown, the pedigree attached to the augmentation of his Grant of Arms shows that he was born in 1768.

Pilfold appears to have had a very slow start in his naval career: having gone to sea about 1781 as a captain's servant – a typical role for a youth hoping to become an officer – he was first listed as a midshipman in October 1788, serving in the East Indies until May 1792 in HMS *Crown* (64) under William Cornwallis. As master's mate in HMS *Brunswick* (74), he was present at Lord Howe's victory on the Glorious First of June (1794) and was commended by his dying captain, John Harvey, to Howe, who promoted him lieutenant and took him into the flagship HMS *Queen Charlotte*.

On 14 February 1795, Pilfold was transferred into HMS *Russell* (74) and took part in the action fought on 23 June off Britanny by Admiral Lord Bridport against Rear Admiral Villaret-Joyeuse, in which three French line-of-battle ships were captured. In the following September, he was appointed to the sloop of war *Kingfisher* (18) as first lieutenant and assisted in the capture of several privateers, mainly on the Lisbon station; on 1 July 1797 he was also instrumental in suppressing (but not without bloodshed) a mutiny.

While in the *Kingfisher*, his appointment in other ships was twice sought by their captains (Sir Hugh Christian of the *Russell* and Sir Charles Pole of the *Commerce de Marseilles*), but there was no one to replace him in the sloop, where he remained until 1798, when he joined the *Impetueux* (74). The highlight of his time in her was the raid on the River Morbihan on 6 June 1800, when, under his direction, boats from the *Impetueux* and four other ships with 300 soldiers burned or captured about a dozen small French warships. His captain's report brought him to some public attention, and when the *Impetueux* was paid off on 14 April 1802 he was her first lieutenant.

During the brief Peace of Amiens, aged thirty-three, he met his bride-to-be, Mary Anne Horner. They married on 20 June 1803, just over a month after the resumption of hostilities between Britain and France, and he was soon appointed to HMS *Hindostan* (54), from which he was moved the following year to HMS *Dragon* (74) and in 1805 to HMS *Ajax* (74), under Captain William Brown. The ship took part in Sir Robert Calder's action off Cape Finisterre on 22 July 1805 – an ill-fated event for Brown, but one which gave Pilfold his greatest chance of naval glory.

The critical response to the Cape Finisterre action led Calder to demand a court martial for himself, and Brown was called as one of his witnesses. Consequently, it was Lieutenant Pilfold, and not Brown, who commanded the *Ajax* at Trafalgar.

In the approach to battle, a marine in the *Ajax* described her sailors as admirably calm, preparing as if for a parade, with some sharpening cutlasses and others dancing a hornpipe, and the many items jettisoned in preparation included six wooden ladders, ten cot frames, six stanchions, a grinding stone, a set of screens for berths, four weather sails, and thirty feet of copper funnelling for the galley stove.

The ship stood sixth in Nelson's column, and if her log is correct, she opened fire quite early, shortly after 1pm, cutting the line a few minutes later. Engaging first the French *L'Intrepide* and then the Spanish *Argonauta*, she played a full part, if not a particularly outstanding one, in the battle, and fortunately suffered only two dead and nine wounded.

Pilfold's real moment of triumph was on Christmas Day 1805 when, jumping the intermediate rank of commander, he was made captain. Naturally, he received the naval gold medal; in April 1808, he was granted an augmentation to his family arms; and in 1815, he was made a Companion of the Bath. But otherwise his naval life after Trafalgar was a decline even longer and slower than his rise. He did not serve at sea again but returned to private life for twenty-two years, during which he did much to support his nephew, the poet Percy Bysshe Shelley, and entered unsuccessfully into farming. He sold up from that in 1824 and with his wife and their two daughters moved from Sussex, his county of birth, to Wales and Devon, and in 1827 – presumably from official sympathy at his financial plight – he was appointed 'captain of the Ordinary' at Plymouth, a care and maintenance post which he held until 1831, when he suffered a stroke and was rendered 'quite childish'. His wife died in 1832 and he, after another stroke, died in the Naval Hospital at Stonehouse, Plymouth, on 12 July 1834. His body was buried two days later at St George's Church, East Stonehouse.

SWRH

Date of death: 12 July 1834
Place of death: Stonehouse, Plymouth (probably in the Royal Naval Hospital)
Where buried: St George's Church, East Stonehouse, Plymouth
Note: Records show that Captain John Pilfold was buried, aged 68 years, at St George's Church, East Stonehouse on 14 July 1832 (Burial Register in Plymouth & West Devon Record Office). The church was sited on West Chapel St, which has  now been renamed Durnford St, at the junction with Emma Place. In 1941, the church was badly damaged in a heavy air raid. It remained in this state, and could not be used for worship, until 1957 when it was decided it would not be rebuilt. It was acquired by the local council and demolished, and is presently the site of a car dealer. The remains of those buried there were removed and re-interred at Efford Cemetery. However there is no record of Captain Pilfold's remains being included among those which were removed.
Therefore it must be concluded that there is now no visible record of the grave on the ground.

WILLIAM PROWSE

(1753–1826)

Captain HMS *Sirius*

William Prowse commanded one of Nelson's frigates, HMS *Sirius*, during the Trafalgar campaign. As part of the detached frigate and small ship squadron commanded by Blackwood, the *Sirius* was one of the 'eyes of the fleet'. On 19 October, the *Sirius* was the closest inshore ship to Cadiz and Prowse had the honour to signal to Blackwood that the Combined Fleet had hoisted sail and were coming out of port. Due to the wind dropping, it was not until the next day that the Combined Fleet cleared Cadiz and the *Sirius* had to sail smartly away to avoid being taken.

William Prowse was born in Stonehouse, Devon, in 1753 and joined the Royal Navy on 13 November 1771 on board HMS *Dublin*, rated able seaman aged eighteen. In 1778, he transferred to HMS *Albion* and was soon made

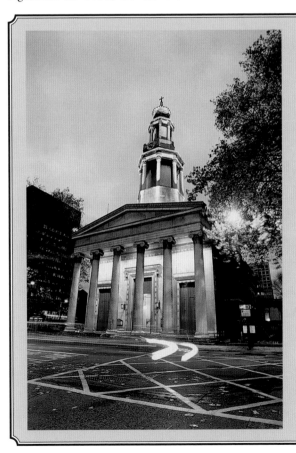

Date of death: 23 March 1826

Place of death: St Pancras, London

Where buried: St Pancras New Church, Euston Road, London

Note: Church records show that Rear Admiral William Prowse was buried in the crypt of St Pancras New Church in a communal grave. There is no plaque inside the Church to him, and so he has no visible memorial. However, it is believed that he lived in Euston Road, and Prowse Place, a quaint cobbled mews in Camden, is named after him. The Church has plans to develop the crypt into a study centre, and if these come to fruition, the human remains there will be exhumed and re-interred elsewhere.

midshipman and then master's mate. He served with distinction during the War of American Independence and passed for lieutenant in January 1782, receiving his commission eleven months later. At the start of the French Wars, Prowse was made sixth lieutenant of HMS *Barfleur* and in that ship took part in the Battle of the Glorious First of June (1794), in which he was severely wounded and lost a leg. On recovering from his wound, he was made master and commander of HM Brig *Raven* and took part in the Battle of Cape St Vincent on 14 February 1797. Following that action, he was involved in the unsuccessful attempt to track and take the huge crippled Spanish four-decker, the *Santissima Trinidad*. Prowse was subsequently made captain of HMS *Sirius* and in July 1805 was part of Sir Robert Calder's fleet which attacked the Combined Fleet off Finisterre. During this action, Prowse boldly tried to take a Spanish treasure galleon but was thwarted by the arrival of the van of the Combined Fleet.

As a frigate, the *Sirius* took no direct part in the Battle of Trafalgar but was stationed on the windward side of the weather column, where she was expected to repeat signals and to assist ships in distress. Just prior to the battle, the fleet's frigate commanders were summoned on board the *Victory* and just as the firing started, Nelson sent them back to their respective ships. However, one account states that Prowse was delayed on board the *Victory* and did not return to the *Sirius* until the battle was over. Following the battle, the *Sirius* took the crippled *Temeraire* in tow.

Following Trafalgar in April 1806, Prowse, still in command of the *Sirius*, spotted a French flotilla sheltering in the mouth of the River Tiber. Despite being heavily outnumbered and out-gunned, Prowse attacked and after a two-hour action captured the French ship-corvette *Bergère* (18). For this action, Prowse was mentioned in dispatches and received a sword of honour from the Lloyd's Patriotic Fund. Prowse was created a CB in 1815, a colonel of the Royal Marines in 1819 and made rear admiral in 1821. He died in London in 1826.

NS

ROBERT REDMILL
(1765?–1819)
Captain HMS *Polyphemus*

Of Robert Redmill, little is known. He joined the Royal Navy at an early age and was made a lieutenant in 1783, so it is estimated that he was born around 1765. During the French Revolutionary Wars, he was promoted commander in 1795 when he gained command of the *Comet* (14). He apparently took part in Admiral Hotham's action of 14 March 1795 when the French attempted to secure Corsica and in the effort lost the *Ca Ira* and *Censeur*, but in Hotham's dispatch there is no mention of either Redmill or his ship.

Redmill was promoted captain in 1796, took command of the *Delft* (64) in 1799 and remained on board until the end of the war in 1802. In 1801, he was

Date of death: February 1819

Place of death: Stevenage

Where buried: St Nicholas Church, Stevenage

Note: Records show that Captain Robert Redmill CB, of Sanders Green, aged 65 years, was buried at St Nicholas Church, Stevenage on 28 February 1819 (Hertfordshire Archives and Local Studies burial register ref D/P 105/1/29). However, a search of the graveyard shows no grave or headstone which can be ascribed to him. This may be because many of them are now so eroded that they are illegible, and the church does not have a full record of them. Therefore it must be concluded that there now remains no visible record on the ground of the grave.

involved in the Egypt campaign when the *Delft* transported men of the Guards regiments. For his services in Egypt, he received the Turkish gold medal from the Sultan, Selim III.

The *Polyphemus* became his ship in 1805 and in her he fought at the Battle of Trafalgar. She was located in the rear of Admiral Collingwood's line and was late into action; she was briefly involved when the *Berwick* turned to follow the *Principe de Asturias* after she had been roughly handled by the *Defiance*. Following the battle, she played a more active role in assisting the *Victory*, which was much disabled and required a tow. Redmill's men managed to get a hawser through the captain's cabin to the bow of the *Victory*, and saw her safe into Gibraltar.

Redmill's naval career ended in 1806 due to ill-health, and he died in February 1819.

SCC

Edward Rotheram
(1753–1830)
Captain HMS *Royal Sovereign*

Rotheram first went to sea in a collier – a far cry from the proud career that he subsequently carved out for himself. At Trafalgar, commanding Vice Admiral Collingwood's flagship, the three-decker *Royal Sovereign*, he had the responsibility of spear-heading the lee column of fifteen ships into the enemy line. Like Collingwood, Rotheram came from Northumberland. Even so, the

Date of death: 6 November 1830
Place of death: Bildeston House, Bildeston, Suffolk
Where buried: St Mary Magdalene Church, Bildeston, Suffolk
Description: The grave is on the lawn on the south side of the Church about 183 cm from the boundary wall. Made of pink-brown marble, all four sides slope upwards to a flat cross at the top. There are inscriptions on the north, south and east sloping sides.
Dimensions: 193 cm x 71 cm x 36 cm high.

Transcription

(South side)
IN MEMORIAM
CAPTAIN E. ROTHERAM, C.B.
WHO COMMANDED
ADMIRAL COLLINGWOOD'S FLAG SHIP
R. SOVEREIGN
AT TRAFALGAR 1805,
WAS ALSO FIRST LIEUT OF CULLODEN
IN LORD HOWE'S VICTORY OF JUNE 1ST 1794

(North side)
DIED AT BILDESTONE HOUSE
6 NOV 1830   AGED 77

THOU HAST COVERED MY HEAD
IN THE DAY OF BATTLE

(East side)
ERECTED BY BROTHER OFFICERS AND FRIENDS
1891

MARBLE PLAQUE

Location: St Mary Magdalene Church, Bildeston, Suffolk, on the south wall of church, some 15ft above the ground, near the choir stalls and St Nicholas' Chapel. By its side flies a white ensign.

Description: Made of white marble, house-shaped, mounted on a black wooden board, and supported by two wooden brackets.

Dimensions: 76cm x 50 cm.

Transcription

TO THE MEMORY OF

Capt **EDWD ROTHERAM, R.N.**

WHO COMMANDED THE

ROYAL SOVEREIGN,

THE LEADING SHIP

AT THE **BATTLE** OF **TRAFALGAR**

HE DIED SUDDENLY AT BILDESTONE HOUSE

AND WAS BURIED IN THIS CHURCH YARD

NOVEMBER 6TH 1830 AGED 77 YEARS.

A BROTHER OFFICER ERECTED THIS TABLET.

EDWARD ROTHERAM

relationship between admiral and captain was initially strained but softened by Nelson's intervention, who invited the two men to dine together with him.

Rotheram was born in 1753 in Hexham and enlisted in 1777. Between 1778 and 1782, he was midshipman, a master's mate and, in HMS *Monarch*, an acting lieutenant serving under Lord Howe. He also served under Howe at the Glorious First of June (1794) as a senior lieutenant on the *Culloden*. This was a stepping stone to promotion to commander that year and to captain in 1800.

At the Battle of Trafalgar, Rotheram was attired for the occasion in an oversized cocked hat, which he claimed he always wore when fighting, and full dress uniform, apparel which no one could make him change.

His ship had been a laggardly sailer, dubbed 'the West Country Waggon', but when she rejoined the fleet a fortnight before Trafalgar she had become one of the most speedy, being newly copper-bottomed. Rapidly in range, Rotheram broke through the Franco-Spanish line astern of the towering *Santa Ana* to engage her with a potent show of gunnery, long before support could come to bear. So powerful was this overture that Collingwood called out to this captain, 'Rotheram, what would Nelson give to be here!' unaware that his Lordship, witnessing the scene from across the water, was saying at almost the same moment, 'See how that noble fellow Collingwood carries his ship into action!'

When Rotheram turned to pull alongside his adversary, his ship had by then attracted the wrath of four other opponents. Help eventually arrived, led by the *Belleisle*, and so the *Royal Sovereign* was able to achieve the submission she wanted after the longest single fight in the whole battle, but at great cost to the crew and ship. In due course, the *Euryalus* took the *Royal Sovereign* in tow and Collingwood transferred his flag to her. Immobilised as his ship was, Rotheram maintained action as the enemy bore down on her and continued to the end of the conflict.

Rotheram then took command of the *Bellerophon* and escorted the *Victory*, with Nelson's body on board, back to England. At the funeral that followed, he carried the guidon. His actions at Trafalgar were rewarded with the naval gold medal and a sword of honour from the Lloyd's Patriotic Fund before he resumed active service in the *Bellerophon* in the Channel and the Baltic from 1805 to 1809.

In June 1815, Rotheram was appointed a Companion of the Bath and was one of the captains of Greenwich Hospital from 1828 for two years. He died on 6 November 1830 in Bildeston, Suffolk.

JRG

William Gordon Rutherfurd

(1765–1818)
Captain HMS *Swiftsure*

Rutherfurd was born in Wilmington, North Carolina, in 1765 and entered the Royal Navy in August 1778 on board HMS *Suffolk* following an education at Edinburgh and St Andrew's University. He served as a midshipman for just over six years and passed for lieutenant in September 1793. He received his lieutenant's commission in January 1794 and served in Vice Admiral Sir John Jervis's flagship, HMS *Boyne* (98), during the British invasion of Martinique in 1794. Rutherfurd commanded a detachment of sailors ashore and led a storming party that captured the important post of Monte Mathurine.

Following this action, Rutherford was made commander in July 1794 and then captain in November 1796. He took part in the capture of the Dutch island of Curacoa in 1800, served for some time in the West Indies and assisted the British blockade of the French Atlantic ports. In 1805, he was appointed command of HMS *Swiftsure* (74) in which capacity he served during the Trafalgar campaign.

The *Swiftsure* was the tenth ship in line in the British leeward column commanded by Collingwood during the Battle of Trafalgar. By the time the *Swiftsure* broke the enemy line, the fight had been going on for several hours and the British ship HMS *Belleisle* was being fired on by three enemy vessels. Passing the completely dismasted *Belleisle*, the crew of the *Swiftsure* gave her a rousing cheer and then poured a devastating broadside into the stern of one of the *Belleisle*'s tormentors, the French ship *Achille* (74). The *Achille*'s mizzen mast quickly went by the board and fire broke out in her foretop. Soon the *Achille* was ablaze and, despite the danger of explosion and the fire setting off the French guns, Rutherfurd sent the *Swiftsure*'s boats, aided by those of the *Prince*, *Pickle* and *Entreprenante*, to rescue as many men as they could. The *Swiftsure* lost two men killed and several wounded during this mercy mission but succeeded in rescuing many of the *Achille*'s crew. Shortly after the *Achille* exploded, killing the remaining crew on board. After the battle, the *Swiftsure* took the French prize, the *Redoutable* (74), in tow. However, as the gale that followed the battle increased, it became clear that the *Redoutable* was sinking and after rescuing as many men as she could, Rutherfurd had the *Swiftsure* cut free. Later, she managed to rescue some more men adrift on spars but the *Redoutable* sank and with her went five of the *Swiftsure*'s crew.

In 1814, Rutherford was appointed a captain of Greenwich Hospital and made a Companion of the Bath in 1815. He died at Greenwich on 14 January 1818 and was buried in St Margaret's, Westminster, where a tablet was erected to his memory.

NS

IN MEMORY OF
WILLIAM GORDON RUTHERFURD, C.B.
CAPTAIN OF H.M.S. SWIFTSURE AT THE
BATTLE OF TRAFALGAR,
DIED 14. JANY 1818.
ALSO OF
LILIAS RUTHERFURD, HIS WIFE,
DIED 5. NOV. 1831.
BOTH BURIED HERE.

Date of death: 14 January 1818
Place of death: Greenwich Hospital
Where buried: St Margaret's Church, Westminster, London
Location: White marble tablet, on the north wall of the Church, under the Admiral Blake window.
Description: A very simple tablet, with text in three colours
Dimensions: 38 cm x 33 cm
Note: The church burial register states that the actual grave lies in the north vault of the church, the same side as the memorial tablet.

Transcription

IN MEMORY OF
WILLIAM GORDON RUTHERFURD, C.B.
CAPTAIN OF H.M.S. SWIFTSURE AT THE
BATTLE OF TRAFALGAR.
DIED 14. JANY 1818.
ALSO OF
LILIAS RUTHERFURD, HIS WIFE,
DIED 5. NOV. 1831.
BOTH BURIED HERE.

John Stockham

(1765–1814)

Acting Captain HMS *Thunderer*

Stockham is amongst the most elusive of the Trafalgar Captains: very few details of his life and naval career are known for certain. Nevertheless, they provide the basis for some interesting commentary.

There were two main branches of the Stockham family, in Wiltshire and in Devon, and in both John was a popular name. This John, one of the Devon Stockhams, was baptised at St Sidwell's Church in Exeter on 24 July 1765 and was commissioned as a lieutenant on 29 April 1797, around the time of his thirty-second birthday. Such a late date is in itself significant. *The Commissioned Sea Officers of the Royal Navy 1660–1815* lists him as having been promoted commander prior to Trafalgar, but gives no date; *The Trafalgar Roll*, in contrast, describes him as still a lieutenant at the time of Trafalgar. But despite the lack of definite data, some probabilities may be defined, and some insight given into his situation on the morning of 21 October 1805.

To become a lieutenant at age thirty-two was unusually late, but while talent and ability helped early promotion, having 'interest' – some influential connection – was of nearly paramount importance, and it seems that Stockham's provincial background lacked 'interest'. To give just one example of the power of interest, Thomas Capel (captain at Trafalgar of the 32-gun frigate HMS *Phoebe*) was eleven years younger than Stockham, but was commissioned lieutenant only twenty-four days earlier than him, then was promoted commander in October 1798 and captain in December 1798; but Capel's rise was helped by the fact that he was the son of an earl.

Even so, any able young officer could bring himself to senior attention by a distinctive contribution in action. Many did, including at least one, Thomas Hardy, whose social background was scarcely more distinguished than Stockham's; but while the still youthful Hardy gained 'interest' through his professional relationship with Nelson and went on to become flag captain at Trafalgar, there is nothing to suggest that Stockham had any comparable opportunity.

Thus it seems plain that if Stockham joined the Navy at thirteen, as did most potential officers, he did not come to early notice for promotion because (unlike Capel) he lacked social connection; and either for the same reason or through sheer bad luck from the competitive situation, unlike Hardy he was not in a position to gain distinction in action before Trafalgar.

Even so, he was clearly a very capable officer, because in 1805 he was first lieutenant of the warship HMS *Thunderer* (74) – not an office given lightly away. So in the context of Trafalgar, it is worth considering what a first lieutenancy meant, and the situation of contemporary senior lieutenants.

Leaving Nelson aside, out of all the Royal Navy officers in command during

Date of death: 6 February 1814
Place of death: Exeter (at his home)
Where buried: St Sidwell's Church, Exeter
Note: Records show that John Stockham, of Holy Trinity Exeter, was buried at St Sidwell's
  Church on 15 February 1814, aged 49 years (burial register in Devon Record Office,
  Exeter). On 2 May 1942, during one of the heaviest air raids on Exeter, St Sidwell's parish
  was devastated, and the church was completely burnt out. The Rector, Rev Narracott, risked
  his life to rescue the church registers and silver from the vestry. The tower was declared
  unsafe, but in 1957 the building was rebuilt. However it is no longer used as a church, and
  has become a community centre.
Only a few gravestones survive in what used to be the graveyard. One of these stones, which
  has now been laid horizontally, appears to show the names of some of Captain Stockham's
  family. It is heavily eroded, but the following is legible

MARTHA

CAROLINE SUSANNA STOC…

WHO DIED…

MARTHA CHAR[ITY] STOC…

WHO… JOHN ….MARTH… .TOC.….

Research shows that Caroline Susanna Stockham and Martha Charity Stockham were sisters,
  whose parents were John and Martha Stockham. They were baptised on 8 May 1812 and
  11th September 1809 respectively. However, we cannot be certain, although it is possible,
  that this John Stockham and the Captain are the same man, as John was a common name
  in the family. It is also possible that this is the Captain's headstone, as there appear to be
  other names recorded on it which are totally illegible.
Therefore, until further research can be undertaken, it must be concluded that there now
  remains no visible record on the ground which can definitely be ascribed to Captain Stockham.

Trafalgar, nine were commissioned lieutenant in 1775–9; ten in 1780–9; and
eighteen in 1790–7. Stockham and Capel were the last two and, as noted, Capel
gained early further promotion. On the day of battle, only six officers in
command were still lieutenants: four (Stockham, Pilfold, Hennah and Cumby)

were first lieutenants of their ships and two (Lapenotiere and Young) had their own small commands.

There was a tendency for a lieutenant to be given, when possible, roughly alternating roles to improve his experience: a third lieutenant in a large warship could move to command a very small one, then return to be second lieutenant, and so on, until reaching the rank of first lieutenant, when he was deemed fit to take full control whenever the captain was not present – as, for example, by cause of death. The first lieutenant was only a heartbeat away from command, and it was nearly impossible for him to be anything less than competent – especially on the eve of a great battle in a unit such as a 74.

First Lieutenants Cumby and Hennah, both commissioned in 1793, took over command in the heat of battle when their captains were killed. Pilfold (commissioned in 1795) and Stockham had rather more notice, taking over when their captains were recalled to Britain to stand witness at Calder's court martial; but of all the British commanders present, Stockham was certainly the most junior.

He was also probably the least experienced in a major command. Thomas Capel, his close contemporary on commissioning, had become his senior in rank, but at Trafalgar commanded a frigate half the *Thunderer*'s size. Moreover, Capel had been consistently in command in the years since his rapid promotion; Stockham had not. And even Nelson had not commanded a 74 until joining HMS *Captain* in 1796, by which time he was thirty-seven years old and a commodore.

When the day of Trafalgar dawned, Stockham was forty years old, acting captain of a major unit, and yet without (as far as we know) any previous comparable command. Given his apparent background of no worthwhile connections but long naval experience, his emotions may be guessed at – some personal fear, and a strong professional understanding of what was expected – and although, like Pilfold in the *Ajax*, he played a comparatively limited role, nevertheless it was valuable: he assisted the *Revenge* and did not shy from engaging far stronger enemy vessels (the Spanish *Principe de Asturias* (112) and the French *Neptune* (84)), sustaining losses of sixteen killed and wounded, including three officers, but without material damage to his ship. Stockham's personal records may be limited, but the wider record speaks well not only for him but also for the Navy's training of its first lieutenants in general.

After Trafalgar, Stockham received the gold medal, the thanks of Parliament and a sword of honour from the Lloyd's Patriotic Fund, and with Pilfold was promoted captain on Christmas Day 1805: both officers were thus given a few days' seniority over Cumby and Hennah, promoted captain on 1 January 1806. Such a fine distinction could have been important on approaching flag rank, but none of them did. Stockham had no further naval career but died on 6 February 1814 in Exeter, where his body was buried at St Sidwell's, the church in which he had been baptised forty-nine years before.

SWRH

CHARLES TYLER
(1760–1835)
Captain HMS *Tonnant*

Tyler had a distinguished career in the Navy in which he saw action in a number of conflicts and during which he became one of Nelson's inner circle. A veteran of the Battle of Copenhagen, where he commanded the battleship HMS *Warrior*, he had previously served with Nelson in the Mediterranean when they were both captains.

Born in 1760, the son of an army captain, he enlisted at the age of eleven and was a lieutenant by 1779. His first captaincy of a number of ships was with the *Meleager* in 1790 in which he saw service at Toulon under Admiral Hood in 1793, and at the reduction of Calvi the following year. He subsequently transferred to the *Diadem* and commanded her at Hotham's action off Genoa in 1795. His next appointment was to the frigate *Aigle* (not to be confused with the French *Aigle*) in which he acquitted himself credibly against privateers before the ship was totally wrecked on Plane island, off North Africa, in 1798. Having survived this ill-fortune, he captained the *Warrior* at the blockade of Cadiz and took part in the Baltic campaign of 1801. He then commanded Sea Fencibles between 1803 and 1805 prior to joining the *Tonnant*.

Tyler's campaign off Cadiz in 1805 began awkwardly when he had to entreat Nelson to intervene on his behalf to extricate his son from domestic disaster. The young officer had jumped ship in Malta and, burdened by debt and love for a ballerina, was languishing in a Naples prison. Nelson did intercede and, unknown to Tyler, offered to pay for the son's release. Earlier that year, Nelson had intervened to save Tyler's son from being removed from the lieutenants' list for his conduct: 'I still hope the young man, who does not want abilities, will recollect himself,' he had told the father.

At Trafalgar, Tyler's ship was positioned three behind Collingwood and his first action was to drive off two of the enemy ships that had crippled the *Mars*. One, the *Monarca*, was so damaged that she struck her colours, but being unable to surrender to the *Tonnant* or any other British vessel, briefly rehoisted her flag. In the meantime, the *Tonnant*'s attention was turned to the second ship, the *Algésiras*. A sharp change of the *Tonnant*'s course resulted in a tangled embrace and a fierce engagement that culminated with a grim loss of life on both sides. The French Rear Admiral Charles Magon was mortally injured and Tyler was also seriously wounded from a musket ball in the thigh, forcing him to pass command to one of his officers. The *Algésiras* having surrendered, Tyler's vessel still had enough fight in her to confront the *San Juan Nepomuceno* which submitted, enabling Tyler to claim her as his prize.

In recognition of his gallant action at Trafalgar, Tyler was awarded the naval gold medal, the Lloyd's sword of honour, and received thanks from a grateful Parliament. He continued in active service and in 1808 he witnessed the surrender of the Russian fleet at Lisbon before passing through a succession of appointments and awards. He was made a KCB in 1815, elevated to GCB in 1833, and served as commander-in-chief at the Cape of Good Hope from 1812 to 1815. He reached the rank of admiral of the white in 1830 and died at the Spa in Gloucester in September 1835.

JRG

Arms of Sir Charles Tyler (from his memorial).

Date of death: 28 September 1835
Place of death: The Spa, Gloucester
Where buried: St Nicholas Church, St
  Nicholas, Glamorgan
Description: Wall monument situated in a
  family chapel on the south side of St
  Nicholas Church. Made of white marble
  mounted on a black background, the
  inscription is surmounted by a partially
  draped urn, and has a coat of arms
  below with the words 'Algeziras',
  'Ildefonso', 'Tria juncta in uno', 'Ich dien'
  and 'My King and Country'.
Dimensions: Approx 180 cm x 120 cm
Sculptor: J E Thomas, London

Transcription

TO THE MEMORY OF **SIR CHARLES TYLER**

OF COTTRELL IN THIS PARISH

ADMIRAL OF THE WHITE AND KNIGHT GRAND CROSS

OF THE MOST HONORABLE AND MILITARY ORDER OF THE BATH

WHO DIED THE 28TH DAY OF SEPTR 1835 AGED 75 YEARS.

HIS LIFE WAS DEVOTED TO THE SERVICE OF HIS COUNTRY

DURING A PERIOD OF THE GREATEST DIFFICULTY AND DANGER

AND HE BORE A DISTINGUISHED PART IN THE EVER MEMORABLE

BATTLE OF TRAFALGAR

IN WHICH HE COMMANDED THE TONNANT 80 GUNS

HE WAS HONORED BY THE FRIENDSHIP OF THE HERO

UNDER WHOSE AUSPICES HE THEN FOUGHT AND IN WHOSE GLORIOUS END

IT WAS NEARLY HIS FATE TO PARTICIPATE

HIS WHOLE PROFESSIONAL CAREER WAS MARKED BY MANY ACTS

OF VALOR AND HONORABLE SERVICE

WHICH WON FOR HIM THOSE HIGH DISTINCTIONS

WHICH WERE CONFERRED ON HIM BY HIS SOVEREIGN

WITH THE GENERAL APPROBATION OF HIS COUNTRYMEN

ALSO OF **MARGARET** WIFE OF THE ABOVE

WHO DIED THE 21ST DAY OF JULY 1835 AGED 76 YEARS

Robert Benjamin Young

(1773–1846)
Lieutenant commanding HMS *Entreprenante*

Robert Young was appointed captain (although still a lieutenant, Young was given the courtesy title of captain) of HMS *Entreprenante*, a 10-gun cutter, and assigned to Nelson's fleet before Trafalgar. Nelson's orders instructing him to join the fleet off Cadiz were written on 14 September, the very day he left England. Young claimed that the day before Trafalgar, Nelson instructed him to keep the *Entreprenante* close to the *Victory*, as he would be given the task of taking home any dispatches regarding the result of the forthcoming battle. In the event, it was HMS *Pickle* that was given that honour and Young was 'mortified' by this decision.

Young was born on 15 September 1773 in Douglas, Isle of Man, the son of a serving Royal Navy officer. He joined the Navy as a midshipman on board HMS *Severn* under the command of his father, Captain Robert Perry Young, in 1781. He passed for lieutenant in May 1791 but did not receive his commission until 1796. In May 1795, Young distinguished himself during the action between the British sloop *Thorn* (16), commanded by Captain Otway, and the French corvette *Courier-National* during a spirited night action that resulted in the capture of the French ship. Young further marked himself out in 1795 when he landed a hundred British soldiers, in heavy surf under enemy fire, on the Island of St Vincent during the Carib war. At the end of the action, he found his hat and clothes had been shot through although he was unhurt.

He was then appointed lieutenant to HM SLOOP *Bonne Citoyenne* (20), as its name implies, a captured French vessel. In this vessel, Young served at the Battle of Cape St Vincent in 1797 where Nelson first became a national hero by taking two Spanish battleships. A few weeks after the battle, Young was injured during an action with a Spanish vessel when part of the *Bonne Citoyenne*'s fore topmast was shot away and fell on him. Young recovered to fight further actions against the Spanish in defending Gibraltar. The *Bonne Citoyenne* then joined Nelson for the campaign against Napoleon in Egypt that culminated in the Battle of the Nile in 1798. Although not present at the battle, the *Bonne Citoyenne* joined the fleet shortly after and assisted with repairs. Young returned to Britain in HMS *Colossus* and survived that ship's wreck off the Isles of Scilly. Young was appointed first lieutenant of HMS *Goliath* and in 1801, during a hurricane in the West Indies, the *Goliath* was laid on her beam-ends and lost her masts. Within twenty-four hours, Young had her back in order and taking prizes, a remarkable testament to his sea-going skills.

Following the Trafalgar campaign, Young continued to serve in the *Entreprenante*, assisting in the blockading of the enemy coastline, but due to ill-health he left the ship in 1807. He subsequently served in a number of vessels and in 1810 was made commander but was then beached and did not serve again. In 1839, he was given a Greenwich pension and he died of heart disease in 1846 and was buried in St James's, Exeter.

The *Entreprenante* was a small ship and as such took no direct part in the Battle of Trafalgar although, seeing the French ship *Achille* on fire, Young sent her boats to rescue as many of her crew as they could. A total of 161 Frenchmen were packed into the *Entreprenante*, a vessel that had a crew of only forty! The *Achille* blew up before more men could be saved. Despite the severe overcrowding and the great storm that followed the battle, Young took the *Entreprenante* in search of the drifting prizes and alerted the fleet to the fact that the crew of the Spanish ship *Bahama* had recaptured that vessel. This action allowed the *Bahama* to be taken again and a valuable prize kept in British hands.

NS

Date of death: 26 November 1846
Place of death: 7 Cobourg Place, Exeter (his home)
Where buried: St James' Church, Exeter
Note: Records show that Cdr Robert Benjamin Young died at his home in Exeter, of heart disease, aged 73 years, in the presence of Mary Young, who was presumably his wife (copy of death certificate obtained). An obituary in the *Gentleman's Magazine*, Feb 1847, states that he left a wife, two sons and two daughters wholly unprovided for, despite having a pension from Greenwich Hospital of £65 pa. The burial register of St James' Church, presently in Devon Record Office, shows that he was buried on 3 December 1846.

The centre of Exeter was heavily bombed on 2 May 1942, as described under the entry for John Stockham, but the location of St James' graveyard has now been identified, thanks to research by Mr John Draisey of Devon Record Office. The original St James' Church, destroyed in 1942, had been built in 1836 near what is now the football ground, but was surrounded by buildings, with no space for a graveyard. However, Mr Draisey discovered that an area of land immediately to the north of St Sidwell's Church was consecrated during 1846, and the eastern portion of this became St James' graveyard, so Cdr Young must have been one of the first to be buried there. However, in 1969 this burial ground was cleared and all human remains were re-interred in the Higher Cemetery, Pinhoe Road. There is no record of any headstone for Young. The land that used to be the graveyard of St Sidwell's and St James is now under the King William Street car park and Wat Tyler House. Therefore it must be concluded that there now remains no visible record on the ground of the grave.

THE TRAFALGAR AWARDS
by Sim Comfort

In the annals of British naval history, there had never been a battle fought on such a scale and with such a decisive victory as Trafalgar, and the country was not hesitant in distributing awards to all those who took part – excepting only the women on board the ships of the victorious fleet. The following is a list of those awards along with comments that, it is hoped, will throw some light on them.

ROYAL AND PARLIAMENTARY HONOURS

As Nelson had already been a viscount, his brother, William, was created an earl. Collingwood became a baron. Northesk was already a peer in his own right and so he was made a knight of the Order of the Bath. Captain Thomas Hardy was made a baronet.

The other captains had to wait until the Order of the Bath was extended in 1815. At that time, those who had reached flag rank were created knights commander (KCB) and the remaining survivors were made companions (CB). Some of those who were created KCB were later elevated to knights grand cross (GCB).

All those who took part received the formal thanks of both Houses of Parliament and Collingwood and Northesk were given state pensions. The new Earl Nelson received an enormous windfall from his late brother's efforts: £5,000 annual pension, £90,000 to purchase a suitable estate and £10,000 to furnish it.

OFFICIAL MEDALS

The King's naval gold medal had been instituted in 1794 to reward the admirals and commanding officers at the victory of the Glorious First of June and it had been awarded for a number of fleet actions subsequently. A similar award was made for Trafalgar. The three admirals received the naval large gold medal and each captain the small gold medal. The frigate captains were excluded, since they were not actually in action, but the two lieutenants commanding battleships, Stockham and Pilfold, both received the medal, and were promoted captain following the action. Lieutenants Hannah and Pryce Cumby, who took command when their captains were killed during the action, did not receive the small gold medal, although they were promoted captain following the action. In these cases, the gold medals went to the families of the deceased captains.

When the Order of the Bath was expanded in 1815, the new knights and companions were supposed to return the gold medal in exchange for the badge of the Order. Very few captains complied with this requirement! The naval gold medal was something very special and bureaucracy was not going to reclaim what cannon and the sword had won.

No official medal was issued to any of the other participants and it was only in 1848 that the government finally agreed to recognise the soldiers and sailors who had fought during the 1793–1815 wars with a silver medal. For the Royal Navy and Royal Marines, the medal bore a bust of the young Queen Victoria on the obverse, and Britannia sitting on a 'hippocampus' on the reverse. Individual clasps were affixed to the suspension, with each clasp recording an action or battle in which the recipient had taken part. Each medal bore the recipient's name impressed upon the rim. By 1848, such was the attrition due to age that only 1,250 applied for their medal with the 'Trafalgar' clasp. Of the captains, only three survived to claim it – Codrington, Bullen and Capel. Capel, who was a member of the Board of Admiralty when the medal was introduced, actually sat on the committee that decided which battles should be commemorated with clasps.

Unofficial Medals

An unnamed pewter medal was issued by the son of the great industrialist, Matthew Boulton, to all non-commissioned officers, seamen and Royal Marines who fought at Trafalgar. Although unofficial, it

was sanctioned by the government. Examples are also known in bronze as trial pieces, bronze gilt as presentation pieces to the Crown and other important people, gold as c1900 re-strikes, and silver. The silver medals were made available only to Trafalgar officers and they had to pay for their medals. Re-strikes continued well into the nineteenth century. It appears that a number of officers decided to buy them to be worn when, in 1848, the Naval General Service medal with Trafalgar clasp was issued. The classic design of the Boulton Trafalgar medal places it amongst the most important Nelson medals struck. Although many seamen were disappointed that the medal was issued to them in pewter, many others greatly prized this gift 'To the Heroes of Trafalgar', and had the medals engraved with their name and the name of their ship, and then had the medal fitted into a glazed case for safe keeping.

Another unnamed pewter medal, rimed in gilt bronze with a ring for suspension and worn on a blue ribbon, was issued privately by Nelson's prize agent and friend, Alexander Davison, to all who had served on board HMS *Victory*. Davison had previously issued a medal to all officers, men and marines who fought at the Battle of the Nile, 1 August 1798, which was the first example of a British medal being issued to all participants of a battle, on land or sea.

Presentation Items

Following a precedent set for earlier battles, the City of London awarded the freedom of the city and the gift of a very fine gold and enamel hilted small sword to both of the surviving admirals, and a silver gilt sword to Captain Hardy. The City of London swords remain among the very finest presentation swords ever produced in Britain.

The freedom of a number of cities was voted to both the surviving admirals and a number of the captains at Trafalgar. The freedom was often accompanied with a fine silver or enamelled presentation box.

However, by far the most numerous presentation items were given by the Patriotic Fund. Established in 1803 by the insurers Lloyd's of London, the fund was primarily designed to provide compensation for those wounded during an action and the dependants of those killed. However, money was also set aside to reward successful captains with either a sword of honour or vase of honour (the captain could choose which he preferred). For Trafalgar, the value of each special Trafalgar sword and vase was set at £100. Both

Top: *Silver version of the Boulton Trafalgar Medal that belonged to Captain Charles Bullen (Sim Comfort Collection)*
Above: *Lloyd's Patriotic Fund sword presented to Captain Charles Bullen.*
Previous page, top: *Large King's naval gold medal awarded to Admiral Collingwood (obverse).*
Previous page, bottom: *Large King's naval gold medal awarded to Admiral Collingwood (reverse).*
Right: *Silver vase presented by the Lloyd's Patriotic Fund to Captain James Nicoll Morris.*

the vase and sword were splendid, to say the least, and the original 1803 design was improved upon to reflect the Battle of Trafalgar. In this instance, the lieutenants who succeeded to command were honoured, as well as the family of a deceased captain. As an example, Cumby of the *Bellerophon* received a Trafalgar sword, and Cook's widow, a silver vase. Lady Nelson was also honoured with a vase valued at £500, and Nelson's brother William, a vase of the same value; Collingwood a vase to the value of £500, and Earl Northesk a vase to the value of £300. Additionally, the captains of the frigates and smaller vessels were also honoured – so, for example, Capel of the *Phoebe* received a vase with a value of £100.

MONETARY AWARDS

Prize money was one of the usual 'perks' of naval service, but Trafalgar was disappointing in this respect because so many of the captures were lost in the great storm that followed the battle. Only four captured vessels survived. Appreciating the problem, the Admiralty established a special fund of £300,000 to be added to the prize value achieved. Every person mustered on board every British ship received prize money. In the end, a captain received £3,362 and an able seaman £6 10s. The share of all those killed was forwarded to their next of kin, although this did not always work as well as it should because this often involved a long drawn-out claim.

The Lloyd's Patriotic Fund also made awards. The sum of £100 was given to each severely wounded and £50 to each slightly wounded lieutenant, captain of marines and other officers of the second class;

£50 for severely wounded and £30 for slightly wounded officers of the third class (warrant officers including the boatswain, carpenter, gunner, master's mate); £40 for severely wounded and £25 for slightly wounded officers of the fourth class (petty officers, mates to warrant officers); £40 to every seaman and marine whose wound was attended with a disability through loss of a limb; £20 to each seaman and marine who was severely wounded, but not disabled, and £10 for each seaman and marine who was slightly wounded. Lastly, 'relief be afforded to the Widows, Orphans, Parents, and Relatives, depending for support on the Captains, Officers, Petty Officers, Seamen and Marines, who fell in these glorious engagements, as soon as their respective situations shall be made known to the Committee.' In addition to the actual money made available, Lloyd's printed a handsome certificate that was addressed to the recipient and sent to them. Considering the killed and wounded numbered around 1,700, this is an astonishing level of generosity from the insurance market.

In addition to the financial and numismatic rewards that men received for participating in this great naval action, they came away with something far more important and that stayed with them during the rest of their lives.

They were with Nelson at Trafalgar.

Sources

Biography

The Oxford Dictionary of National Biography
The Naval Chronicle
Allen, Joseph, *Memoirs of the Life and Service of Sir William Hargood* (London 1861)
Broadley and Bartelot, *The Three Dorset Captains at Trafalgar* (London 1906)
Kennedy, Ludovic, *The Band of Brothers* (London 1951)
Mackenzie, Col Robert H, *The Trafalgar Roll: The Ships and the Officers* (London 1913 – reprinted Chatham Publishing 2004)
Murray, A, *Memoirs of the Life and Services of Admiral Sir Philip C.H.C. Durham* (London 1846)
O'Byrne, William, *A Naval Biographical Dictionary* (London 1849 – reprinted Vintage Naval Library 1997)
Robinson, William, *Jack Nastyface* (London 1836 – reprinted Chatham Publishing 2002)
White, Colin, *The Nelson Encyclopaedia* (Chatham Publishing 2002)
Wyndham-Quinn, *Sir Charles Tyler, GCB, Admiral of the White* (London 1912)

The Battle

Bennett, Geoffrey, *The Battle of Trafalgar* (London 1977)
Clayton, Tim, and Craig, Phil, *Trafalgar: the Men, the Battle, the Storm* (London 2004)
Clowes, Laird, *The Royal Navy: A History* (London 1897–1903) Vol 5
Corbett, Julian, *The Campaign of Trafalgar* (London 1910)
Cordingly, David, *Billy Ruffian (the story of HMS Bellerophon)* (London 2003)
Desbriere, Edouard, *The Naval Campaign of 1805: Trafalgar*, translated and edited by Constance Eastwick (Oxford 1933) 2 vols
Fraser, Edward, *The Enemy at Trafalgar* (London 1906 – reprinted Chatham Publishing 2004)
Gardiner, Robert (ed), *The Campaign of Trafalgar* (Chatham Publishing 1997)
Howarth, David, *Trafalgar, The Nelson Touch* (London 1969 – reprinted 1997)
Jackson, T Sturges (ed), *Logs of the Great Sea Fights* (London 1990) Vol II
James, William, *The Naval History of Great Britain* (London 1837) Vol 4
Legg, Stuart (ed), *Trafalgar: An Eyewitness Account* (London 1966)
Maine, Rene, *Trafalgar, Napoleon's Naval Waterloo* (London 1957)
Nicolas, Sir Nicholas, *The Dispatches and Letters of Lord Nelson,* (London 1846 – reprinted Chatham Publishing 1998) Vol VII
Pope, Dudley, *England Expects* (London 1955 – reprinted Chatham Publishing 1998)
Schom, Alan, *Trafalgar Countdown to Battle 1803–1805* (London 1990)
Terraine, John, *Trafalgar* (London 1976)
Tracy, Nicholas, *Nelson's Battles* (Chatham Publishing 1996)
Warner, Oliver, *Nelson's Battles* (London 1965)
White, Colin, 'Nelson's 1805 battle plan', *Journal of Maritime Research*, 2002, www.jmr.nmm.ac.uk

Nelson Monuments

Fraser, Flora, 'If you seek his monument' in Colin White (ed), *The Nelson Companion* (Stroud 1995; new edition 2005)

ILLUSTRATION SOURCES

John Curtis: 38

Dean and Chapter of Westminster Abbey: 27, 82, 114

David Hilton: 78

Dean and Chapter of Westminster Abbey: 27, 82, 114

Franklin Grigg: 81

National Maritime Museum, London: 38, 64, 112, 123, 125

The Naval Chronicle: 47, 56

Matt Prince: 21, 24, 25, 27, 28, 29, 31 (bottom), 32, 34, 35, 37, 39, 40, 42, 43, 44, 47, 49, 50, 51, 54, 55,
    58, 59, 63, 66, 68, 71, 72, 74, 76, 77, 79, 83, 85, 87, 91, 93, 95 (bottom), 98, 99, 100, 102, 104, 106,
    107, 109, 110 (bottom), 116, 119, 120

Royal Naval Museum, Portsmouth: 12, 17 (top & bottom)

Doreen Scragg: 66

Sim Comfort Collection: 20, 30, 45, 124 (top & bottom)

Warwick Leadlay Gallery: 22, 26, 69, 89, 103

The two illustrations on pages 88 and 118 are from private collections.

The two plans on pages 8–9 and 18–19 drawn by Michael O'Callaghan

Inside front cover: Tombstone of Redmill. (Matt Prince)

Inside back cover: Memorial to Rotheram. (Matt Prince)

ADDENDUM

Name: Sir Thomas Fremantle
Date of death: 19th December 1819
Place of death: Naples
Where buried: Naples, on 23 December, with full military honours. The site of the grave was unknown
    until January 2005 when Cdr Charles Fremantle discovered in Buckinghamshire Record Office,
    Aylesbury, a note of the funeral expenses which describes the location 'nel giardino del Dott Sigr
    Carlo Califano fuori Porta S Gennaro' [in the garden of Don Carlo Califano outside the gate of San
    Gennaro]. This area been identified as the garden of the monastery of San Carlo all'Arena which
    had been used as a non-Catholic burial ground since 1529, on payment of a fee to the monks, as
    City ordinances prohibited the burial of non-Catholics within the city walls. The site of the
    monastery was immediately outside the walls of the city in front of the Porta San Gennaro, and
    next to the church of San Carlo all'Arena which is still standing today on via Foria. In 1799 Califano
    bought the garden and continued to run the cemetery as a business for non-Catholic burials, until
    in 1826 the Consul, Sir Henry Lushington, established the 'English Cemetery' at Santa Maria
    delle Fede.
There is now nothing left of the garden, and four schools occupy the area.
Thanks are due to the present British Consul, Michael Burgoyne, and to Carlo Knight, for much of
    the above information.

THE 1805 CLUB

President: Mrs Lily McCarthy CBE
Honorary Chairman: Peter Warwick

Founded in 1990, the Club has three main objectives:

- To assist in the preservation of monuments and memorials relating to Vice Admiral Lord Nelson and seafaring people of the Georgian era;

- To promote research into the Royal Navy of the Georgian period, and especially of Vice Admiral Lord Nelson;

- To organise cultural and historical events.

Since its foundation, the Club has been responsible for over forty-five projects. These range from major works – such as the erection of a new monument to Emma Hamilton in Calais and the installation of new plaques in the Painted Hall at the Old Royal Naval College Greenwich to mark the spot where Nelson and Collingwood's coffins lay in state – to more straightforward restorations of the tombs of Nelson's wife Frances and his daughter Horatia.

The Club has also published a ground-breaking series of monographs on Nelson's battles, incorporating all the latest research. Additionally, its annual journal, *The Trafalgar Chronicle*, is now recognised as a major source for new research on Nelson and his Navy.

Membership is open to all who are interested in promoting the Club's aims and it already has many members overseas, including a strong contingent in the USA. A membership form is available online at the Club's website, or can be obtained from: The Membership Secretary, The 1805 Club, 81 Pepys Road, West Wimbledon, LONDON, SW20 8NW

The Club maintains a website, where further details of its activities may be obtained: www.admiralnelson.org.

THE TRAFALGAR CAPTAINS MEMORIAL PROJECT
Instituted in 2003, the project is The 1805 Club's main contribution to the bicentenary of the Battle of Trafalgar. The project's aim is to locate, record and, where necessary, restore the graves of all those who commanded ships, or flew their flags, at Trafalgar.

The project is administered by a special committee:
Colin White – committee chairman and publication editor
John Curtis – club and committee secretary and archivist
Peter Warwick – club chairman, PR and website
Chris Gray – fundraising
Graham Simpson – project surveyor
John Kerr – project architect